December 27, 1971

On the occasion of your second anniversary — so happy to be sharing it with you.

Jamie and Genie

Peachtree Street, U.S.A.

Books by Celestine Sibley

Peachtree Street, U.S.A.

AN AFFECTIONATE
PORTRAIT   *by Celestine Sibley*
OF ATLANTA

PHOTOGRAPHS BY
KENNETH ROGERS

Doubleday & Company, Inc., Garden City, New York.

For Jimmy, Susan, Mary and Muv, who love it too.

Contents

List of Illustrations

Following page 72

Following page 168

Peachtree Street, U.S.A.

Why Do We Love It?

CHAPTER I

A few years ago the police picked up an elderly and eccentric Atlanta citizen on complaint of her neighbors that she was throwing rocks at and using what the law fastidiously referred to as "opprobrious words" to passing children.

It was a hot August day and the old lady wore not only a wool dress but a heavy winter coat to cover it. When the police matron made her undress for the routine delousing shower, it was discovered that she also wore, tied here and there about her person in little cloth bags, $10,500 in cash.

"Loony," said the officers who happened to know that she had been subsisting for years out of Broad Street garbage cans.

"Yeah," agreed the police matron sympathetically. "She doesn't belong here. She belongs in Milledgeville State Hospital."

"Milledgeville . . . don't be absurd!" put in the old lady crisply. "I'm not that crazy and I'm not going a step. It's too far from Peachtree Street!"

The consummate logic of that position very nearly convinced the police and the Lunacy Commission which later
examined the old lady in Ordinary's Court.

Odd she undeniably was. But insane? She obviously had a
sufficient hold on her faculties to recognize one truth which
is fixed and immutable in the minds of all clear-thinking
citizens. And that, of course, is this: Only a lunatic would
voluntarily and for any length of time leave Peachtree Street.

Why do we love it?

Not for itself alone, surely. There are more beautiful, more
exciting, more interesting thoroughfares in the world. We love
it because Peachtree Street symbolizes in our minds and in
the minds of people all over the world a city called Atlanta,
Georgia.

And why do we who can't even get together on whether we
are Atlantans or Atlantians (the Atlanta *Constitution* and the
Atlantan Hotel insist on the former; the Atlanta *Journal* and
the Federal Penitentiary hold out for "ian") . . . why do we
lustily and with one accord proclaim Atlanta's superiority
among the cities of the world?

The question engrossed Scarlett O'Hara back in 1862.

"Why was the place so different from the other Georgia
towns? Why did it grow so fast? After all . . . it had nothing
to recommend it—only its railroads and a bunch of mighty
pushy people. . . . Like herself, the town was a mixture of
the old and the new in Georgia, in which the old often came
off second best in its conflicts with the self-willed and vigor-
ous new. Moreover, there was something personal, exciting
about a town that was born—or at least christened—the same
year she was christened."

To those of us who were born and christened somewhat

later and who followed her on to Peachtree Street from older cities in the South and younger cities in the North, from small towns and farms and country places, Atlanta is the same—personal and exciting.

Its very newness is challenging. It hasn't had time to settle into any mold, to grow set in its ways. There's room for all. In fact, there's a welcome for all, the kind of welcome that frontier communities must have held out to all new settlers: Come, bring your ideas and your energy to add to ours. Your tools, your axe and your shovel, your strength and your daring, your laughter and your learning . . . we can use you!

In a way Atlanta is even now, in the 118th year of its age, a frontier town—the spiritual capital of what Henry Grady called and what continues to be, the New South. It is the last encampment of those who recognize the South itself as still a largely unexplored, undeveloped land. It has venturesomeness and the large tolerance of youth. It has confidence without the self-contained smugness of older, more insular cities.

Not so many years ago Atlanta *Constitution* columnist Harold Martin (now an associate editor of the *Saturday Evening Post*) thought up a brief and disarming answer to people who sometimes lengthily—and windily—disagreed with him. It sums up Atlanta's attitude toward both outside critics and those blessedly "pushy people" who move in with mighty ideas and monstrous big plans.

This answer:

"Dear Sir, You may be right."

So often critics and newcomers have been right that it behooves Atlanta to be receptive of new knowledge, new talents, new money. At the time of her greatest travail, when her existence was spectacularly threatened by a torch-toting Yankee named W. T. Sherman, Atlanta entrusted to another Yankee—a New Englander named L. P. Grant—the task of fortifying the city.

Although the fortifications didn't stop Sherman, Atlanta recognized the fault did not lie in the planning and engineering skill of Colonel Grant and in gratitude for his services the city named a park for him. (Visitors sometimes are misled into thinking that Grant Park may have been named for Ulysses S. Grant but Atlanta is not *that* tolerant!)

There's nothing new about the fact that Yankee money has long made the economic wheels turn in the South. (Most of us southerners grew up without knowing there was any other kind of money!) But Atlanta, unlike many older, more truly Deep South cities, does not take money with one hand and use the other to bar admittance to its more sacred social and cultural institutions.

Just as it entrusted its fortifications to a Yankee in 1860, today custodians of our most cherished traditions and history are citizens who happen to have been born in the North. The executive director of the Atlanta Historical Society, Colonel Allen P. Julian, was born and grew up in Indiana. Author of the most authoritative and comprehensive history of Atlanta—a hefty, three-volume tome called *Atlanta and Environs*—is another gentleman from Indiana, Franklin M. Garrett. Accepted authority on the Battle of Atlanta and technical adviser on the film *Gone With the Wind*, as well as Disney's *Song of the South* and *The Great Locomotive Chase*, is Wilbur Kurtz, who came from Illinois.

This same happy acceptance of newcomers has given Atlanta the name among older southern cities of having a bumptious, *nouveau riche* society. Again Atlanta smiles sunnily and says: "Dear Sir, You may be right."

No matter what we have of money and breeding, Society's most universally accepted commodities, nobody forgets for a moment that Atlanta also has Mrs. Mulligan.

According to history Mrs. Mulligan was Atlanta's first arbiter of taste and manners. She gave the first party ever held in Atlanta and wrested and held for her day the leadership of Atlanta society.

Mrs. Mulligan was the wife of the foreman of one of the crews engaged in hacking a railroad right-of-way through the forest to the town which was in that year of 1839 called Terminus, forerunner of Atlanta.

Mr. Mulligan was considered a valuable man but he wouldn't stay on the job unless his wife joined him and Mrs. Mulligan wouldn't set foot in the wilderness settlement unless the rough cabin assigned to her had boards put over its dirt floor. So the railroad builders, complaining at the loss of precious man and mule hours, took a team off the road and sent it miles to a mill to haul two loads of puncheons and laid Mrs. Mulligan a floor.

Mrs. Mulligan was gracious—Mrs. Mulligan was hospitable. She moved in and promptly gave a ball to which everyone was invited.

"It was a *crème de la crème* affair and the function established Mrs. Mulligan as the leader of the Four Hundred," John J. Thrasher, the railroad builder, later recounted in an interview with the Atlanta *Constitution*. "She was quite a fine-looking woman of strong physique and if anybody had questioned her leadership, could have established her claim to the championship as well as the leadership."

Following Mrs. Mulligan's lead the other railroad wives demanded plank floors for their shacks. The trapped railroad builders could but comply. Living conditions were improved, social activity was facilitated and the pattern for Atlanta society must have been set. For it continues true today, more than a century later, that spunk, spirit, resourcefulness and that Mulliganesque quality called personality hold their own handily anywhere Atlantans gather for any reason.

"Personal . . . exciting," Scarlett called our town. Latter-day chroniclers are inclined to put down as Atlanta's four chief claims to distinction a sheeted band of terrorists, a bottled drink, a great golfer and Margaret Mitchell's big book. They are usually listed in this order: 1) Ku Klux Klan; 2) Coca-Cola; 3) Bobby Jones; 4) *Gone With the Wind.*

These phenomena tell something about the town, to be sure. But they don't tell why it is personal and exciting to great masses of people who never met Bobby Jones or a Klansman, who haven't read *Gone With the Wind* and who drink buttermilk by day and bourbon and branch water by night.

I think it's the weather—the wonderful, terrible, capricious, never-the-same weather, brisker and cooler than anywhere else in the South or than in most northern cities because of its altitude (1050 feet) but moist and benign enough to nurture a green forest of trees and a year-round succession of blooming flowers and shrubs.

I think it is the way Atlanta smells—factory smoke and

coffee roasting and the poignant summertime fragrance of magnolias blooming in the parks and around Capitol Square. I think it's the smart, pretty, going-places look of the women and the way men still take off their hats in elevators—even the fast, crowded, thirtieth-floor express elevators.

I think it's the young secretaries and Georgia State College co-eds tanning their legs in downtown Hurt Park at lunch-time and the carillon in the steeple of Trinity Methodist Church playing "Abide with Me" at dusk. I think it's the big stores with their escalators and fashion shows and bargain days and their individual and strictly local special events. Davison's lovingly tending three potted peach trees, as proof that there *are* peach trees on Peachtree Street, or annually giving up all its show windows to the Southeastern Art Exhibit and its sidewalks to smocked and bereted artists from the Atlanta Art Institute. Or the crowds jamming Forsyth Street on Thanksgiving night to see the lights go on on Rich's big skyborne Christmas tree and to hear the carols sung from the store's glass bridge by the town's biggest choirs.

I think it's a four-alarm fire on a winter night in a town that was destroyed by fire once, nearly destroyed again and that remembers with a sharp sense of tragedy the Winecoff Hotel holocaust of 1946.

It's Alabaster Alley in Buttermilk Bottom and Shakerag Road and Coca-Cola Place and all the fashionable northside residential streets that got their names from grist mills or old Chattahoochee River ferries. It's a rainy January and the General Assembly convening on Capitol Hill. . . . Noon-time on a summer day and the millworkers from Fulton Bag and Cotton Mill resting on tombstones in Oakland Cemetery. It's the sound of pneumatic drills constantly, unceasingly tearing up downtown streets . . . the shrill cry of a stream-lined train heading north in the night . . . the smell of the stockyards, the bawl of a yearling calf that will be sold at auction tomorrow . . . the clucking of a helicopter making its shuttle run to the airport and the whine of jet airliners cutting across the sky to the north, south, east and west.

It's a Georgia Tech football game on a Saturday afternoon, an all-night "gospel sing" in the Municipal Auditorium, Big Bethel's white-robed, golden-winged Negro choir, led by a Satan in red-satin tights and cape singing "Hand Me Down My Silver Trumpet, Gabriel" when they present the allegory, *Heaven Bound* each year.

It's the tulip festival, a St. Patrick's Day parade, a funeral by Patterson. It's WSB signing off with "Dixie." It's neck bones and pig tails and souse meat on sale at the Municipal Market . . . the opulent, summertime richness of water-melon and sweet corn and peaches and tomatoes at the State Farmer's Market. It's traffic jams and parking tickets and policemen whistling like meadowlarks.

It's Roland Hayes singing the spiritual of his slave grand-father on the stage at Atlanta University and it's Bessie Smith's "Down in Atlanta G-A, under the viaduct everyday . . . drinking corn and hollerin' hooray . . ." pouring out of a Decatur Street record shop.

Personal. Exciting. And something else that is paradoxical and very moving to me. Although for many years a disfran-chised capital city from the standpoint that Georgia's county unit system made the urban areas practically voiceless in state politics, Atlanta is a country town, a Georgia country town. Probably more than any other great metropolitan city in America (population a million, area 128 square miles) Atlanta draws its strength, its character and its flavor from the land.

Set a little north and west of the center of the biggest state east of the Mississippi, Atlanta has reared against the sky its tall buildings and factory smokestacks, has crisscrossed the earth with railroads and millions of dollars of expressways and has filled the air with the mighty roaring of winged traffic from Army and Navy bases, a jet bomber plant and the fifth busiest airport in America.

And yet it hasn't lost the oneness, what the old hymn called the mystic sweet communion, with the red clay hills, the rolling fields and forests, the mountains and the piny woods which gave it life. Certainly the economy has something to do with this. Despite the influx of industry in recent years, Georgia continues to be predominantly agricultural and what affects farm folks affects the folks in its capital city.

But I believe it's closer to the heart than to the pocketbook. I hear country in the speech of my neighbors—the turn of a phrase, the lapse into the quaint Elizabethan English of the hill country by a clerk in a store or a cultivated, Ivy-League educated guest at a party. I see it in the way Atlanta people trek to all parts of the state to participate in the old rural rituals and celebrations.

Camp meeting time in Georgia was historically a season when crops were laid by and families hitched up the horses, tied the family milk cow to the back of the wagon and drove to Salem or Shiloh, Smyrna or New Hope camp ground for a week or two of spiritual refreshment—daily preaching and singing—and physical and mental refreshment—feasting and reunioning with friends and relatives. It hasn't changed much. Oh, the "tents," those rude shacks that usually encircle the open-air tabernacle at most camp grounds, may have acquired a coat of paint and an electric stove. And the wagon with the chairs in it has given way to a Cadillac or a Chrysler. But Atlantans still go by the thousands to camp meeting in the summertime.

Three or four of the old camp meeting grounds flourish practically within the city limits.

Atlantans, as most Georgians, are predominantly Methodist or Baptist by upbringing and proud Bible-Belters all. And each summer you'll find many of them packing lunches and going back to the "homecomings" and the Decoration Days of the little country churches where they or their ancestors worshiped. While cicadas or the "July flies" make a summertime symphony in the oak trees overhead, these urban citizens spread dinner on the grounds with their country kin and wander about the old cemetery, rereading the inscriptions on headstones, placing store-bought city flowers on the old graves.

Religion isn't all that ties Atlanta to the country. Anything that happens in Rising Fawn, Georgia, or Social Circle or Dewy Rose or Ty Ty or Talking Rock is news in Atlanta. The two Atlanta newspapers maintain a statewide network of correspondents and keep staff members on the road constantly covering the tobacco market in South Georgia, livestock and poultry production in middle and North Georgia, rose queens and camellia queens and cotton queens and even such improbably entitled belles as Miss Gum Spirits of Turpentine.

In the fall when the Blue Ridge Mountains blaze with crimson and gold, Atlantans go northeast to Hiwassee to the mountain fair to buy sourwood honey for their table and patchwork quilts for their beds. They stir up the dust on the unpaved roads going northwest to Plum Nelly (so called because it's "plum out of Tennessee and nelly out of Georgia") to look at Miss Fannie Mennen's clothesline art exhibit and to eat gingerbread and drink apple cider.

Sure Atlanta has its country clubs, its symphony orchestra, its art galleries, its annual season of the Metropolitan Opera Company. But until recently its business and professional leaders still met for lunch regularly at Ed Venable's Restaurant for potlicker and crackling bread or fried fatback and hominy.

It has a full complement of millionaires—the Coca-Cola kind and others. It has debut parties and white-columned mansions—antebellum atmosphere with postbellum air conditioning. An inland city, it has one of the biggest yacht clubs in America; but on their way to Lake Allatoona to play with their boats, members pass at the edge of the city limits a two-room log cabin where old Jim Whitley lived until 1960 in exactly the same way as his grandfather, who built the cabin in 1840.

We have our nightclubs and a sprinkling of foreign restaurants, occasional French and Italian movies. The town may have hooted derisively fifteen years ago when "Ol' Gene" Talmadge grazed a cow on the lawn at the Governor's Mansion and invited his country constituency to drop by anytime and share a pitcher of buttermilk with him. But some of those who laughed were pleased to accept an invitation to lunch from L. O. Moseley, the late manager of the state-owned Henry Grady Hotel, on the days when he had his chef cook up a batch of chitt'lings or roast a possum.

Naturally the old lady didn't want to go to the State Hospital for the Insane because it *is* "too far from Peachtree Street."

She went—eventually. Such little eccentricities as foraging for food in garbage cans and catching rainwater to drink while hoarding $10,500 in cash on her person and twenty-five pianos she couldn't play in her house, were certainly acceptable. But throwing rocks and those opprobrious words at children . . . *after all!* Atlanta is notoriously mushy-headed about its children, holding them dearer than churches, Cokes and dogwood trees.

So the old lady went from Peachtree Street but not until after lengthy hearings in Fulton Superior Court and not until considerable public sentiment had risen yeastily in her defense.

Margaret Mitchell, the little novelist who brought such renown to Atlanta, was one of those who gloried in the public clamor in behalf of the raffish old eccentric.

It was evidence, she said, that her beloved hometown had not overreached itself and become a too-big city. It proved that Atlanta, small-town fashion, retains an affection and a tolerance for the independent, tough-minded, *odd* citizen who, in the country parlance, is "turned funny."

Struck down and fatally injured by a taxi driver, Peggy Mitchell has gone from Peachtree Street herself. And although her town is splitting its britches to be a big city, I don't think she would be disappointed in it. Atlanta is not only tolerant of the "turned funny"—it *is* turned funny. Individual, exasperating, sometimes ridiculous, it has all the endearing, surpriseful qualities inherent in the natural-born "character."

Love it? I'm crazy about it!

Everything's Peachtree

CHAPTER II

The young major who got on the plane in San Francisco had made the night horrible for the owl flight passengers. He was, as he loudly and unnecessarily assured everybody, "just a Georgia boy who will take a drink." With every mile his accent thickened and sugared like cane syrup cooked overlong and he noisily proclaimed his allegiance to Georgia in general and Atlanta, Georgia, in particular.

"Finest place on the face of the earth and I ain't gon' never leave it no mo'!" he announced.

The two young stewardesses, unable to shush him, gave him a wide berth because the sight of them set up a lot of "Georgia peach-you all" talk which grew increasingly wearisome.

"A professional Georgian," the tired gray-haired man next to me said as he punched his pillow and tried unsuccessfully to shut out the strains of "Ah'm a ramblin' wreck from Georgia Tech an' a helluva engineer!"

"Oh, he's just a homesick war hero," I offered placatingly.

"Maybe," said my neighbor, "but I bet a dollar he's from Ohio or Pennsylvania."

Sleep was impossible so I volunteered to find out. The young man welcomed me with glad cries about southern hospitality, apologies that he didn't have "Ol' Gabe," the Negro butler handy to serve me a mint julep and invited me to join him in heisting the University of Georgia's stirring "Glory, Glory to Old Georgia."

Then I knew my seat-mate was right.

A native Georgian is either a Tech supporter or a Georgia (University of) supporter but never both. This man was filled with the kind of all-encompassing loving-kindness which is common to first-generation Atlantans and football fans who, poor things, had to go "off" to school. (Off is anywhere north of Vanderbilt or Washington and Lee.)

Before the first pale light of dawn presaged the coming day the young major had made a manful confession. His benighted parents, a couple of rich but deserving midwesterners, had waited until he was fifteen years old to move to Atlanta! He had, for reasons beyond his control, gone "off" to school and then to the Army and to Korea. But he was going to make it up. He was going to take his stand at the corner of Cain and Peachtree Streets and spend the rest of his natural life "watching the Georgia peaches go by."

I comforted him as best I could by assuring him that he was practically a native son. Only twenty-five percent of Atlanta's population have the edge on him and me of having been born here. The rest of us have to make up for not being natives by being thrice-zealous converts.

The young officer went to sleep and I went back to my seat. My neighbor stirred drowsily and smilingly received my report.

After a moment he said shyly, "If you're awake when we cross the Alabama line, would you mind punching me? I always like to be watching when home land is sighted."

I grinned and he went on defensively, "Maybe you haven't noticed, but from the air Atlanta is one of the prettiest cities in the country. All those green trees and the red earth. I just happen to prefer earth that's got some color to it, that's all. After all the pallid country I've been over it's a relief to see land that's decently red."

I nodded solemnly and he turned his face to the window. Then he turned back.

"Uh . . . 1923 . . . from Michigan," he said.

This incident illustrates a couple of things about Atlanta: 1) The allegiance, sometimes tryingly loudmouthed, of even her adopted sons; 2) The shiny-eyed pride with which settlers, both old and new, keep *looking* at the town. It is, I sometimes think, as if we were parents measuring with our eyes the growth and the bonny bloom of a child.

Compared to older cities Atlanta has a great scarcity of tourist attractions. Even the most doggedly determined guidebook toter and plaque reader would be hard put to acquire aching feet or eyestrain "doing" Atlanta. This perturbs Atlantans not at all. We conscientiously tick off our "sights" for visitors— the Cyclorama, Stone Mountain, the Wren's Nest, a Minié-ball-battered gas streetlight which burns day and night, symbolizing the "eternal flame" of the Confederacy, the Civil War museum at the Atlanta Historical Society and a few others. But we can't really feel apologetic that our town's bag of tourist tricks isn't larger, any more than a parent can apologize because his beautiful, gifted, industrious daughter isn't also a ventriloquist and a tightrope walker.

We find Atlanta's workaday charms arresting enough. Any day of the week wherever strangers meet, at bus stops or on trolleys, in lounges and bank or post office lines, you hear the questions: "Have you seen . . . ?" "Did you notice . . . ?"

It might be the new window boxes on the Citizens and Southern Bank, the face-washing they're giving the Henry Grady monument, the way the bulldozers are uprooting the woods around another Peachtree Road estate or the newest downtown skyscraper.

We are a community of sidewalk superintendents, kibitzing enthusiastically at every hole in the ground, every convocation of helmeted steel workers, surefooted and lordly, high above our heads on the raw ochre ribs of a new building.

In the spring we are bemused by dogwood, the pristine dogwood which edges streets and driveways with an immaculate ruching of starched blossoms and which stars rich man's garden and poor man's winter-drab backyard with whiteness. We organize tours and motorcades and stage, but never settle, side debates over whether this street in Druid Hills has a better show than that street in Ansley Park.

In the fall we busy about looking at the autumnal foliage, which surely shows a wider range and a greater depth of color *this* year than ever before! Not so many years ago the Botanical Gardens Association of Fulton County held a beauty contest for trees and awarded metal plates to be attached to the trunks of the winners. This engendered a new kind of snobbery. People who would never think of bragging about their membership in the Piedmont Driving Club or that their daughter was Maid of Cotton, brag shamelessly that their sweetgum tree snagged top deciduous honors. An elderly West End widow of my acquaintance, who always considered that her banal bungalow was redeemed by the most glorious maple tree in town, was so miffed at losing "finest" to a Buckhead maple, that she sold out, married a patent medicine salesman and moved to an apartment.

When interest in building palls (or in wrecking, which is a constant and equally fascinating show), when things are quiescent with the trees, Atlantans may shift their attention —but they're still looking.

This could be because a town so complex, so capriciously laid out, presents a challenge to the eye. It's so many different towns, tall upon the hills, sprawling along the Chattahoochee River, running underground on rails and granite-block streets, spilling over into four counties. In 1957, *Fortune* magazine presented a survey of well-run American cities, listing Atlanta's long-time mayor, William B. Hartsfield, as one of the nine outstanding mayors in the country, and giving our town top place in areas of noise abatement and regional planning.

That planning bit was especially sweet to Atlanta ears because, although we're crazy about planning, spending many hours in committee meetings, zoning sessions and traffic engineering conferences, we have some of the most flagrantly unplanned streets in the world.

The downtown thoroughfares were once old Indian trails or cow paths, winding leisurely along ridges, dipping down at springs and coming together at a swift-flowing artesian well which was drilled in the '8os to supplement the town's water supply. The artesian well has since been plugged up; the flagpole which was erected in its place has been removed. A wide area in the middle is Five Points, where skeins of traffic are perpetually knotted and snarled, where most parades are reviewed, many civic campaigns are launched, where the air raid sirens and the New Year's firecrackers sound the loudest.

It is the nominal, although not the actual, center of our city and, of course, part of the language. A loudmouth is somebody who would "tell it at Five Points." A politician who has nothing to hide or, in the recent phrase, a record "as clean as a hound's tooth," is one whose career has been as accessible to the public as Five Points. People have paid off their bets by trundling their opponents in a wheelbarrow through Five Points. The ultimate in public embarrassment, in raw exposure, is summed up in the phrase "like being caught buck nekkid at Five Points."

Actually Five Points is a sedate-looking junction—the center nowadays of the financial section with banks and office buildings presenting a dignified and perhaps a little dull façade to the world. Flowers bloom in boxes on the traffic islands and there's no trace of town pump atmosphere, little tangible evidence that this was the site of the first rude huddle of country stores in 1836, that where the tall William-Oliver Building now stands, Thomas Kile, grocer, had the honor of housing the first municipal election in 1848; that the First National Bank occupies the site of the old Jacob's Pharmacy where in 1887 a citizen with a headache turned Coca-Cola from a tonic to a beverage.

Only old-timers remember that here the horse cars once loaded and unloaded, that a young lawyer named Woodrow

Wilson passed here on his way to his first law office two blocks away, that Presidents have paraded here and peace celebrations centered here and such returning heroes as Bobby Jones, golfdom's grand slammer, have been welcomed here.

Sometimes somebody writes a letter to the editor bemoaning the passing of such Five Points institutions as Pitts' Cigar Store and Sweet Shop which once faced Peachtree Street between Decatur and Edgewood Avenue. Pitts' closed in 1926, but the chocolate sodas he dispensed over his big square marble counter from 1894 to 1926 live on in memory.

Atlantans are prone to refer to the corners that jut out from Five Points as the points of a star—a figure which has been modified and carried on by the Community Planning Council and the Georgia Power Company in a recent survey which depicts Atlanta's expressway system as a starfish, reaching out into a trade area of eighteen counties and drawing workers from a radius of a hundred miles.

But that is a planned star—or starfish—a product of traffic engineering with landscaped parkways and on-purpose greenswards and limited access. This other one, the one that chance and the moccasined feet of the Creek and the Cherokee laid off, is the one at heartbeat level, the one of teeming foot traffic, of intimate sounds and sights that are distinctively Atlanta.

Nobody agrees where Peachtree ends. Some mileage-minded people say it turns north a distance of seventeen miles, becoming, in due course, Peachtree Road and then Peachtree Industrial Boulevard, but I know Atlanta men who give smiling credence to the story which was told to them as little boys—that Peachtree Street runs to New York City.

Its beginning is more settled. A block south of Five Points

there's a man-made island of green grass, towering magnolias and almost constantly blooming borders known as Plaza Park. At the edge of the park there's a peach tree and a small marker to inform the interested that at this spot the old stagecoach road to White Hall Tavern, now a street called Whitehall, ends and Peachtree Street begins.

This is upperdeck Peachtree Street. There is another. Beneath the pavement of street and sidewalk and the hauled-in earth of the little park lie the railroad tracks, which shaped and ordered so much of Atlanta's history and geography, including the start of its most famous street.

No visitors and only a limited number of citizens know this down-under world of granite-block streets, iron rails and black-faced dusty buildings. By day it is the freight entrance to downtown stores and office buildings and is alive with the movement of trucks and trains, of whistling workmen swinging boxes and crates about. Shafts of sunlight shimmering with dust motes sift down around viaducts and alleyways to illuminate it by day. At night it is illy lit and deserted. Commerce relinquishes its hold on this world and it is taken over by derelicts, by drunks and doorway sleepers. "Bus Stop Bill," a bleary-eyed citizen whose profession is mooching carfare, comes home from a hard day at the bus stops with a bottle of muscatel for his stomach's sake and an exciting evening of eluding the police patrol on its regular pickup journeys through the area.

Despite its sinister appearance there's little crime down here. The old winos and rummies who regard it as home are not quarrelsome. They ask only to be let alone, a snug cranny against the winter rain or cold, the comfort of the musty, tomblike chill when summer heat bears down on the pave-ments above. Garbage trucks rumble by, punctuating but not disturbing their rest. Wharf rats grow bold and come out of hiding. Trains, moving at slow, yard speed, with their shrill, anguished cries and their glaring Cyclops eyes of light are no more to the citizens of Atlanta's Down Under than a freight whistling through his cornfield is to the farmer sleeping beside his wife beneath a sun and clover scented counterpane.

This part of Atlanta isn't on the Gray Line tour. It isn't something hosts think of when they want to show the city to a visitor, but it is there and has been growing since 1852 when the city began building bridges—called viaducts locally—over the railroad gulch. Each year a new building or so goes up, extending the steel and concrete roof over another hundred yards or so of tracks and warehouse area.

Plaza Park was the city's first attempt to cover the gulch with beauty and except for the ventilators that stick out at intervals in the grass and shrubbery, there's no sign that this blooming square is really one whopping big dish garden, instead of a park planted firmly on the earth. It may vibrate a little when trains pass beneath it but that could be the fall of water in the big fountain or the flurry of activity among the pigeons, who share the lunch of many downtown office workers.

The pigeons' peanut and popcorn dispensing friends are the despair of the City Parks Department because the salt from the refreshments they scatter on the lawn keeps killing the grass. That's a year-round problem. Their special seasonal one is answering phone calls the day after Halloween when some wag always puts bubble bath in the fountain and it sends beautiful, Technicolor bubbles soaring dreamily through the chill October sunshine, breaking against dark old buildings, dipping in and out of traffic.

If you want a logical, overall, comprehensive picture of Atlanta, Plaza Park or of course Five Points is the place to start. At least that's what Atlantans *say*. Actually few local citizens have a logical overall, comprehensive picture of our town. We get lost driving the cleaning woman home or trying to circle the block to pick up a friend in front of the Red Rock Building.

Atlanta, as many far travelers have observed, may be the only city in the world where it's possible to go around the block and never in due course return to your starting point. A standard, old settler joke about the residential section Ansley Park might well apply to any part of town. That's the one about the man who took a cat out to abandon him and then, hopelessly lost himself, had to follow the cat home.

But we've had our moments of trying to be like the organized cities and line up streets in a tidy fashion with numbers for names. Witness that small wedge of territory in the northeast section where the streets march along in numerical order . . . almost. Starting at Third Street—don't ask me what happened to First and Second!—they are resolutely numbered for maybe a dozen blocks before wholesale skipping sets in. The number notion begins to go to pot before you find Twentieth Street—I don't think it's to be found but then I've only lived in the neighborhood since 1946—and is abandoned entirely at Twenty-eighth Street.

This is confusing to orderly minds but it doesn't upset Atlantans unduly because where it's weak on consistency it's strong on Peachtree—and as any visitor in town for a day can't help noticing, Atlantans like to call as many streets as possible Peachtree. For example, part of what should have been Ninth Street is called Peachtree Place; Thirteenth Street wears that number on one sign and on another is designated as West Peachtree Park. All in all there are twenty-odd streets with Peachtree worked adroitly and not so adroitly into their names.

In spite of this civic capriciousness and the Peachtree fixation, a pattern does emerge, willy-nilly, for those who begin at Five Points earnestly endeavoring to get some idea of how the town looks.

The five streets converging there are named Peachtree (of course!), Whitehall, Edgewood Avenue, Marietta and Decatur.

Peachtree heads north through the better-looking business district, hotel and theater district. It nips along through many old and new community centers, such as Tenth Street, Garden Hills and Buckhead, crosses Peachtree Creek, passes Oglethorpe University, Veterans Administration Hospital 48 and the exclusive Peachtree Golf Club and emerges at the edge of a little town called Chamblee in a welter of gleaming new-style industrial plants. Once famed as a boulevard of beautiful homes Peachtree now has more office buildings, apartment houses, drive-in groceries and Dairy Queen bars than handsome residences. But it is the thoroughfare that cuts closest to the whole northeast and northwest area where houses like baronial halls are set in the midst of wooded acres as tenderly clipped and groomed as parks.

Peachtree's other end, Whitehall Street, meanders south through a busy section of chain shoe stores and dress shops, Kress and McCrory and W .T. Grant stores, credit furniture stores, secondhand shops and eventually warehouses and transport truck terminals. It ends at the Central of Georgia railroad tracks, but if you cross the tracks and continue the same general direction on another street you come to West End, an old section where many prominent Atlantans once lived, Fort McPherson, headquarters for the Third Army, the industrial-minded community of East Point with shirt factories and potato chip plants and next door to it the spruce suburban community of College Park, home of the preparatory school, Georgia Military Academy. Nearby, a mile or so to the southeast, is the little town of Hapeville and Atlanta's Municipal Airport.

Back at Five Points, Edgewood Avenue heads southeast through a stone and steel thicket of office buildings. It passes the Hurt Building (named for a pioneer developer) and exquisite little Hurt Park, overlooked by the marble-faced Municipal Auditorium and a cluster of buildings—some shining and ultramodern and one a barnlike, only slightly remodeled parking garage—which constitute the city campus of Georgia State College, Atlanta's branch of the state university system. Moving along, Edgewood passes the old Municipal Farmer's Market, the largest single retail center for farm products in the state, blocks of small stores and garages, some of them Negro-run establishments branching out from the main Negro business street, Auburn Avenue, which runs parallel to Edgewood. It ends in Inman Park, one time a fashionable collection of homes of Atlanta's horsecar-traveling tycoons, now an area given over largely to boarding and rooming houses.

Marietta Street, the widest of the five thoroughfares, runs northwest from Five Points. It is the old route to Atlanta's smaller but older neighbor, the town of Marietta in Cobb County. A four-lane highway, built during World War II to handle traffic to the big Bell Bomber Plant (now Lockheed) is now a faster, more direct route, but old Marietta Street is busy with local traffic and colorful. From Peachtree it moves past the Henry Grady Monument and the Federal Reserve Bank through a community of wholesale houses, neighborhood shopping areas, textile mill villages, the railroad yards, stockyards and packing houses. Crossing the Chattahoochee River, Marietta Street enters Cobb County as the Old Marietta Road and moves at a more leisurely pace through such pretty communities as Smyrna (the Jonquil City), the town of Marietta itself and eventually Kennesaw Mountain, where there is now a national park and battlefield museum and where Civil War historians gather to retrace the course of fighting leading up to the Battle of Atlanta.

That leaves Decatur Street, of the five streets which converge at Five Points.

For the record, Decatur Street picks up where Marietta Street leaves off and like Marietta Street was once the principal road to an older town which gave it its name, Decatur in De Kalb County. (This is east and in the general direction of Stone Mountain, a great glob of granite and a wonder to be dealt with more fully later.) Now there are better ways of getting to Decatur, and this street—as famous in its way as its glossier neighbor, Peachtree—has other things to commend it than where it's going.

Decatur Street is blues town, the home of the famous "81", the Negro theater where Bessie Smith and her "Liberty Belles" got their start—a street of pawnshops and fish markets, of wholesale grocers and secondhand stores, of root and herb doctors and love potion merchants. There were until recently horribly overcrowded slum apartments for both white and Negro on this street, and there are still hardware stores where you can buy kerosene lamps and iron washpots, and at least one haberdashery (George Pierce's) which lives up to its slogan, "We Cater to Cranks," by stocking outsize and out-of-style furnishings such as button shoes and Hoover collars.

That old Victorian pile, the Kimball House, with its cupolas and squat little iron-lace balconies, once the biggest hotel in the South, was on the corner of Decatur and Pryor Streets. Built in 1885, replacing another Kimball House which was burned in a spectacular fire, this seedy old landmark was torn down a few years ago to make way for a parking garage. Once the gathering place for Atlanta society, the place where visiting Presidents were entertained, the site of the inaugural balls and meeting ground for state political figures going back to Reconstruction Days, the old hotel had come down in the world. Its final guests ran to transients or aging residents who either remembered its days of glory or hadn't much money and needed to do a little light housekeeping and perhaps keep a refrigerator in the hall.

The police station is also on Decatur Street. The new big Grady Hospital is just a block off it on Butler. There's a Decatur Street Merchants Association and from time to time movements to "clean up the place" but, happily, they usually stir it up only temporarily.

Slum clearance and that omnivorous monster, parking, recently razed a few blocks of old buildings, but Hungry Corner —a traffic island at the intersection of Decatur and Central Avenue—still functions. Here Negro men gather daily, waiting to cadge a bit of casual employment, loading or unloading a truck at some nearby warehouse or wholesale outlet. Citizens who have been stood up by their regular yardman or window washer or who need brawn to move a refrigerator or a piano from room to room, simply drive to Hungry Corner and slow down and they are instantly overrun by a swarm of would-be workmen. Some of these are old winos newly out of jail and not much use to anybody, but some, surprisingly, are young and able-bodied laborers who could get steady jobs elsewhere but prefer the variety and suspense of cadging jobs on Hungry Corner.

There was an effort by disciples of conformity years ago to rename Decatur and Marietta Streets East Main and West Main Streets, respectively. Atlantans resisted that at the top of their voices.

As recently as 1929 someone proposed that Decatur Street be called East Marietta Street. A columnist of that day, Loyd A. Wilhoit, snorted: "I'd as soon think of changing Frisco's Chinatown to 'Daisy Dell' or New York's Fifth Avenue to 'Sunnydale'!"

Which shows you. For a young city with youth's enthusiasm for tearing up and remaking things and youth's eagerness to conform, Atlanta can be surprisingly stubborn in its loyalty to the old. Main Street, indeed!

Along Came Sherman

CHAPTER III

"You think we're crazy on the subject of Peachtree?" The old settler asked the question of a visitor. "Sir, I'll tell you something. This town was sired by an iron horse but its dam was a *peach tree*! Remarkable union, remarkable offspring."

The speaker picked up his cane and limped off the bus at the Capitol City Club, chortling appreciatively at his own joke and leaving the baffled tourist just where he was, leafing dispiritedly through Mr. Gilmore's *Street Guide*.

He didn't explain but history does.

Even before a New Hampshire Army engineer drove that stake in the ground in 1837, marking the beginning of a new kind of American city—a lusty, brawling little railroad town—there was a peach tree here. It was a tough and brave peach tree which by some magic found its way inland from the cultivated orchards of the coast and came to bloom and bear

fruit on a strange high mound on the edge of the Cherokee
Nation.

So phenomenal was the presence of a peach tree in the
wilds along the Chattahoochee River that from time to time
skeptics have tried to explain it away by saying that what
Indians called Standing Peachtree was really just another big
old resinous pine or "pitch tree."

If that's right, the soldiers who built and manned the fort
there during the War of 1812 were even worse spellers than
the War Department archives indicate because they called it
Fort Peachtree *at* Standing Peachtree and the road connecting
it with Fort Daniel in Gwinnett County thirty miles away
was named—what else?—Peachtree Road!

Because Atlanta is such a young town a lot of its history has
the freshness of word-of-mouth telling. Until 1903 George
Washington Collier, who was here when the Indians were and
long before the railroad men, could give eyewitness account of
the early days.

He was a plain-spoken old farmer who lived in the woods
north of Atlanta for eighty years, long enough to see his fields
and vast woodland acres become high-priced urban real estate.
He died a rich man, leaving a large family of descendants to
enjoy positions of wealth and leadership in the upstart town
which had followed him to the woods, yapping at his heels
and shattering his solitude.

A *Constitution* reporter who went out to interview him in
1894 quoted the old man as saying, probably irascibly:

"Towns? Towns? Why there were no towns here when I
came. There was nothing except land lots and trails and corn
patches. There was no money. There were no railroads, no
papers. We didn't get the mail but once a week. There wasn't

any business to do, much. The farmers just made their corn and ate it for bread, that was all."

Wash Collier didn't try to substitute the unbelievable peach tree with the mundane "pitch" tree. He said he saw the peach.

"Standing Peachtree was right where Peachtree Creek runs into the Chattahoochee—right where the pumping station is now. . . . There was a huge mound of earth heaped up there, big as this house, maybe bigger, and right on top of it grew a big peach tree. It bore fruit and was a useful and beautiful tree. But it was strange that it should grow on top of that mound, wasn't it?"

Maybe the seed was brought in by some Indian trader circulating between the Cherokee and Creek Nations. Maybe that stern-visaged old Indian fighter, Andrew Jackson, refreshing himself with a lunch from his saddlebag, dropped the seed there. Perhaps an Indian squaw had it in her small pouch of kernels and planted it along with the corn one spring.

Whatever the explanation, Atlanta was identified by a beautiful, fruitful tree long before Georgia caught the national railroad fever and sent right-of-way crews forth in 1837 to find the spot at which a state-authorized railroad, to be built south from Tennessee, could pass around the mountains and head for the rich cotton country and the seaports to the south.

The railroads came in, bringing a new kind of life to Wash Collier's woods and the isolated country where a farmer named Hardy Ivy had erected a log cabin and started breaking the land. Crews of Irishmen felled trees and cut through the hillsides and built fills to make way for the Western and Atlantic first and then the Monroe Railroad and by the start of the Civil War three other railroads, the forerunners of the fifteen main lines of eight systems which make Atlanta the largest railroad center in the South today.

They threw up their crude shacks, their saloons and their rough country stores. All kinds of people followed the railroads and it's no wonder that some of the citizens of Decatur and Marietta looked askance at what was happening at the settlement the railroads had spawned.

There were prophecies of every stripe, but two cherished ones are recorded in Franklin Garrett's *Atlanta and Environs* in his chapter on the 1830s. Alexander Hamilton Stephens, who was to become Georgia's beloved "Little Aleck," U. S. Senator, Vice-President of the Confederacy and later Governor, visited the southeastern terminus of the W. & A. Railroad as a young man of twenty-seven. He is said to have looked on the near-wilderness and cried: "What a magnificent inland city will at no distant date be built here!"

The other prophecy is attributed to a Decatur citizen, Dr. Chapman Powell, who, unlike many of his neighbors, thought the railroad might be an advantage to a community instead of a noisy, dirty nuisance. To a colleague in the legislature who predicted that the terminus of the railroad would "never be any more than an eating house," Dr. Powell retorted: "You will see the time when it will eat up Decatur!"

Decatur hasn't exactly been consumed, but it has grown accustomed to finding itself referred to as a part of Greater Atlanta. By 1851 Atlanta was four times the size of Decatur and had taken a chunk of Decatur's De Kalb County to make itself a brand-new county. With typical frontier thoughtlessness nobody remembered to make note of *why* the name Fulton was picked for the new county and historians are probably destined to remain in eternal disagreement. Franklin Garrett was inclined to favor Hamilton Fulton, the chief state engineer who was a member of the first railroad survey party, but after weighing the contemporary evidence he reluctantly concluded that the honor belonged to Robert Fulton, inventor of the steamboat. Dr. N. L. Angier, a native of New Hampshire, is credited with having chosen the name for the new county and Historian Garrett thinks it likely that Dr. Angier was more impressed by the man whose invention made the *Savannah* the first steamship to cross the Atlantic than by an obscure railroad surveyor.

But there's no doubt as to where Atlanta got its name—from the railroads, of course.

Called first "the terminus" and then Terminus and finally incorporated under the name of Marthasville (for the daughter of Wilson Lumpkin, one of the railroad builders and an ex-governor of Georgia), the little town was rechristened Atlanta in 1845 in a high-handed gesture from a railroad man.

Richard Peters, superintendent and resident engineer of the finished portion of the W. & A. Railroad from Augusta to Covington, had the job of announcing the opening of the road from Covington to Marthasville and for some reason the name Marthasville didn't suit him. Martha's father later said it was "the low voice of envy," but whatever prompted the change, it was no trouble for the railroad to make it.

Mr. Peters asked the chief engineer, J. Edgar Thompson, who was later to become president of the Pennsylvania Railroad, to suggest a better name.

"Western and Atlantic," mulled Mr. Thompson. "Atlantic masculine, Atlanta feminine. Eureka . . . Atlanta!"

The railroad adopted it, the town followed suit and the legislature promptly ratified it. Then everybody spent the next

few years explaining to literary-minded newspaper editors elsewhere that it *was* Atlanta and not a typographical error. They
naturally thought the rambunctious little town must have
been named for Atalanta, goddess of fleetness and strength!

At any rate Atlanta was on its way. The '40s and '50s
were years of almost phenomenal growth when the population, as one early visitor wrote, was "constantly augmenting."
Even then, when its streets were red mud, and roving livestock its main traffic problem, Atlantans were pleased with
their town. Dr. George Gilman Smith, the Methodist minister and historian who came to Atlanta in 1847 as a child,
quoted a bit of rhyme extolling the town's virtues:

> *Atlanta, the greatest spot in all the nation,*
> *The greatest place for legislation*
> *Or any other occupation—*
> *The very center of creation.*

Oddly enough this fulsome praise of the place stuck in his
mind along with the recollection of typhoid fever as a fairly
common summer complaint, the civic project to get the
stumps out of the streets and the really precarious fight staged
by law-abiding citizens to keep the town government out of
the hands of a frontier-style underworld. Drunkards, gamblers,
cock-fighters and idlers lived in Snake Nation (now Peters
Street), Murrel's Row, a section of shanties on Decatur
Street, and Slabtown, a community of huts thrown up on Decatur Street out of slabs from Jonathan Norcross' mill. These
"baddies," organized as the Free and Rowdy Party, stole a
small cannon, relic of the War of 1812, from Decatur where
the townspeople shot it off on the Fourth of July and other
celebratory occasions, brought it to Atlanta, loaded it with

gravel and mud and opened fire on the store of the Mayor, Jonathan Norcross.

Along with the litter on his front porch they left a note warning him that if he didn't resign his post his store would be blown up. The Mayor promptly issued a call for law-abiding citizens to rally. There were secret meetings on both sides, some hand-to-hand combat, but the villains were arrested, thrown in the log calaboose, which they promptly overturned and escaped, and arrested again.

The communities of Snake Nation and Slabtown were burned down and what Dr. Smith called "vile women" who "visited their paramours in the daytime without shame" were hauled out of town. (Franklin Garrett reports that they were taken "nearly to Decatur," which, being but eight miles away, didn't exactly constitute complete banishment even in that day of slow travel.)

Dr. Smith, who reminisced about his childhood in a series of articles printed in the Atlanta *Journal* sixty years later, like a good Atlantan did not let any of the unfavorable aspects of those early days blind him to the innate charm of the place.

He wrote: "I never saw more beauty than there was in the springtime in the groves all over Atlanta. All the undergrowth except the azaleas and the dogwoods had been cut out. The sward was covered with the fairest woodland flowers, floxes, lilies, trilliums, violets, pink roots, primroses—a fairer vision than any garden of exotics show now. Honeysuckles of every beautiful hue, deep red, pink, golden, white, were in lavish luxuriance. The white dogwood was everywhere; the red woodbine and now and then a yellow jessamine climbed on the trees. When a stream was found it was clear as crystal. I have

seen few things so fair in this world of beauty, as were the
Atlanta woods in 1848."

Property values even then started climbing. Land on Peachtree Street which had been worth a couple of dollars an acre
when Hardy Ivy bought a land lot for $225 in produce in
1833, had gone up fast. By 1852 when a Massachusetts
heavy machinery manufacturer named Joseph Winship (great
grandfather of Robert Winship Woodruff, president of the
Coca-Cola Company and one of the richest men in the world)
wanted an acre for a homesite he had to pay $580 for it.

That particular acre happened to be where the Paramount
Theater was until 1960. When Mr. Winship was ready to sell
it in 1866 after Sherman had been through, he was able to get
$15,000 for it. Asa Candler bought it in 1909 for $97,000;
Forrest and George W. Adair paid $120,000 for it two years
later and in 1919 when it was leased out for the building of
the Paramount it was valued at $625,000. Three years ago
that little chunk of Hardy Ivy's old farm changed hands for
$900,000.

The coming of Sherman, of course, was Atlanta's moment
of high drama in history. The railroads which sired the town
now shaped its destiny. As a transportation center it was
valuable to the Confederacy and therefore twice valuable to
the Union.

Colonel Allen P. Julian, the Indiana-born secretary of the
Atlanta Historical Society and curator of its museum at 1753
Peachtree Street, N.W., has been making speeches for years
that nearly provoke a new intramural Unpleasantness by contending that Atlanta, backed up by the rest of Georgia, was
far more important strategically, economically and morale-
wise to the Confederacy than any other southern city . . .

even that one in Virginia. Citizens of Richmond give Colonel Julian the most back talk, but anybody who really wants to make an issue of it is invited to drop by the Historical Society out on Peachtree Street, where the Campaign of Atlanta, which lasted from May to September of 1864, is refought almost daily, round by round, with the help of maps, photographs and stacks of documentary evidence.

Except for a solid core of experts in the Atlanta Historical Society, the Civil War Round Table and a few hobbyists who devote their Sundays and holidays to tramping over battlefields, the average Atlantan's idea of that great campaign is Vivien Leigh and Clark Gable and a great big noisy fire. Details of the battle, although highly regarded by military strategists near and far, are inclined to go fuzzy for native sons and daughters who have trouble remembering just where some of the picturesquely named hot spots of '64 are. Lickskillet, for instance, and Big Shanty and Rough and Ready.

Oddly enough, the people who can go to these places with the unerring instinct of a homing pigeon, knowing that Lickskillet is on the west side, out Gordon Road, Big Shanty was the old name for the town of Kennesaw at the base of Kennesaw Mountain and Rough and Ready is the little community called Mountain View out near the airport, are those transplanted southerners turned Confederate, Colonel Julian, Artist Wilbur Kurtz and Historian Garrett!

However, when a local son or daughter takes up local history it's surprising what a richness of material is available to make his study as interesting, as warmly personal, as a tale told by a grandpa who was there or an old aunt who parched corn for coffee and defied Sherman's marauders from the smokehouse door. That's where most of the material comes from, of course—from the people who were there. Old diaries and letters and bits of family lore gave Margaret Mitchell her start.

Now another generation from the source, it is necessary for historians to sift more carefully the word-of-mouth accounts. Some stories have been beclouded by the passage of the years, some embroidered. The Atlanta Historical Society cautions students against believing that Sherman slept in the upstairs bedchamber and stabled his horse in the front hall of every antebellum house in the vicinity. This is a favorite story.

"If Sherman had slept everywhere in Georgia he is said to have slept," suggests Colonel Julian, "the war would have had to have ended differently. He wouldn't have had time for any fighting."

Far from sleeping away that summer of '64, Sherman considered it a holy crusade to wipe out Atlanta as one of the enemy's chief military depots and manufactories and to "chastise a forward and erring people and turn them from following after false leaders and prophets."

It took him awhile and he didn't quite pull it off single-handedly since the Confederates themselves destroyed everything of military value with every inch of ground they gave. The National Cemetery at Marietta with the headstones bearing the names of Ohio, Indiana and Massachusetts companies, attests to how much it cost him. And in spite of the bitter fighting, the shells bursting around them, the departure of the Confederate forces and the arrival of the enemy, many women, children and old men of Atlanta clung stubbornly to their homes until they were removed bodily by soldiers.

Students of the campaign usually begin at May 1, 1864, with General Sherman and approximately 100,000 well-equipped Union soldiers and 254 guns at Chattanooga and the Confederate General Joseph E. Johnston and his 50,000 not so well-equipped men and 187 guns fourteen miles south at Dalton.

Atlanta, eighty-five miles from Dalton, was Johnston's supply base and, according to Garrett, "full of machine and railroad shops, foundries and arsenals." Grant's instructions to Sherman that spring were to "move against Johnston's Army, to break it up and to get into the interior of the enemy's country as far as you can, inflicting all the damage you can against their resources."

General Johnston, with the familiar hill country and streams to help him, fought a defensive battle which even his enemy, Sherman, found flawless from a military standpoint in the years after the war when such things were considered impartially. He held on to Dalton for twelve days and then retreated eighteen miles south to positions he had prepared at Resaca, where there was bitter fighting for a couple of days. But it was not all fighting, according to the old-timers who were there. At dusk, I have heard them say, the men of both sides settled in for the night.

"You could hear the bugler on the Yankee side start to play," an old lawyer told me. "He would play 'Yankee Doodle' and presently across the river you'd hear a southern boy strike up with 'Dixie.' And then as it got dark and the stars came out, one or the other of them would start 'Home Sweet Home' and the other would join in. They'd play along together in a way that made you want to cry—even more than all the shooting and dying in the daytime."

Johnston retreated slowly and souvenir hunters today find in the fields and woods north of Atlanta sad mementos of

such battles as the bloody four-day affair in Paulding County
—the one Confederates identified as New Hope Church but
which the Federals, whose losses were tremendous, called
"Hell-Hole." There's a national park and museum at Kennesaw Mountain where tourists and Sunday picnickers sometimes drive in their station wagons and get the attendants on
duty to show them how the battle lines were drawn, while
the children look at the pitiful tattered old uniforms and have
their pictures taken on the funny, old-fashioned little cannons.

Historians say that politics and no mistake of Sherman's
was responsible for the slaughter of so many Federal soldiers
at Kennesaw and at Cheatham's Hill. Lincoln, running for
re-election, needed a Federal victory to bolster his policy of
continuing war—and Sherman made the rash and ill-advised
frontal assault in an effort to wrest that victory. That was on
June 27, and less than a month later on July 17, politics on
the other side, the Confederate side, effected the replacement
of the patient, watchful General Johnston with that colorful
one-legged fighting man, "the gallant Hood of Texas."

Johnston, about to be flanked, had withdrawn from Kennesaw Mountain. The fighting was edging closer to Atlanta and
the Confederate President Jefferson Davis and his chief of
staff, General Braxton Bragg, were alarmed in Richmond. It
may have been a strategic withdrawal, but to those men at
that moment in history it looked like the crafty, patient old
Joe Johnston didn't want to fight. The fact that he was out-
numbered two to one apparently didn't matter.

General John B. Hood took over, and under orders to "turn
back the Federals before they reach Atlanta" he seized the of-
fensive, hurled his tired, badly equipped forces at the enemy
at Peachtree Creek and suffered a crushing defeat. A marble

marker at Peachtree Road opposite Brighton Road commemorates the day, July 20, 1864, when 4796 gray-clad soldiers died in defense of Atlanta.

The enemy's foot was on Peachtree Road and coming closer on the south and the east. The first shell had fallen on Atlanta, striking at the corner of Ellis and Ivy Streets and killing a little child.

From then until August 9, Atlanta was a city under siege, and yet strangely enough the citizens went on with life as usual. Some of them dug shelters in their backyards and when the shelling was bad they sought refuge underground. The wounded were pouring into town and food and medicine were hard to get. But Samuel P. Richards, who founded Atlanta's oldest business, the Richards Paper Company, wrote in his diary on August 1, 1864:

"Nothing much of importance transpired during the week that we are aware of. We have had shelling semi-occasionally but thus far none of the deadly missiles have reached our house and we could look upon them at a safe distance with composure. For fear that they should ever reach us I have done several days' hard work preparing a pit in our cellar to retreat to for shelter. One shell pierced the top cornice of our store and went into Beach & Root's building opposite. . . . Our garden is helping us a great deal these hard times. . . . It is to be hoped the contest will not be prolonged indefinitely for there is nothing much to eat in Atlanta though if we keep the R.R. we will not quite starve, I trust."

Mr. Richards recorded that the shelling had ceased by August 25, and that there was a rumor that the enemy was retreating. "It is now known that they have deserted their camps around the city and are going somewhere, but what is their design is hard to tell. I fear that we have not yet got rid of them finally but they have some other plan in view to molest and injure us. But in the meantime we can rest in security for a while, safe from shells. . . ."

The reason for the let-up in shelling Atlanta was soon learned. Sherman's forces had put the Atlanta and West Point Railroad out of commission at Red Oak and Fairburn to the west of town and cut Hood's last supply line, the Macon and Western at Rough and Ready on the south side.

By 5 PM on September 1, Hood's army was evacuating the city, stripping gardens of every edible thing as they marched and singing the sad ballad "Lorena." By midnight no Confederate soldiers were left except a few assigned to blow up the ammunition trains and destroy seven locomotives and eighty-one loaded cars—a job which took them five hours. (Movie demolition crews worked on it for weeks when seventy years later they re-enacted the scene for *Gone With the Wind.*)

Mayor James M. Calhoun and a committee of citizens formally surrendered the city to Brigadier General William T. Ward, the nearest general officer, the next day and within a week Sherman had settled in, setting up headquarters in the handsome, white-columned John Neal home, where the City Hall is today.

While the Yankee soldiers had taken over in Atlanta and were tearing down many fine residences to use the lumber to make Army quarters, Hood was hanging around outside planning to try to draw Sherman north again by striking at the W. & A. Railroad which was now used to bring in supplies for the Federals. Here at Palmetto, a little town twenty miles west of Atlanta, President Jefferson Davis and two staff officers paid Hood a visit, reviewed the troops and were serenaded in the evening by the 20th Louisiana Band.

But Hood didn't succeed in drawing Sherman far from Atlanta. The wily Yankee firebrand left the Tennessee campaign to General George H. Thomas and returned to Atlanta to prepare for his march to the sea.

Before he left he ordered the destruction of what remained of the city's industrial and railroad plants. Four to five thousand residences, churches and stores also burned, either accidentally or by overzealous soldiers. Sherman's soldiers, well provisioned, sang as they left Atlanta.

In his memoirs the Yankee general told of riding out Decatur Street to the strains of the Battle Hymn of the Republic played by a 14th Corps band while the marching men sang:

"John Brown's body lies a-mouldering in the grave."

A week later a state militiaman, sent by Governor Joseph E. Brown to inspect the city, reported a scene of desolation. Thousands of carcasses of dead animals lay in the streets; rubble and ashes were all that remained of fine homes. Blackened stumps instead of shade trees, twisted iron fragments where there had been humming industry, the cemetery looted of small pieces of statuary, headstones overturned, coffins robbed of the silver nameplates and Yankee dead placed in some of the vaults!

A priest, Father Thomas O'Reilly, who had nursed the wounded and dying of both armies during the siege of Atlanta, had appealed to the Federal authorities and managed to save his own Church of the Immaculate Conception as well as four Protestant churches—Central Presbyterian, Second Baptist, Trinity Methodist and St. Philip's Episcopal.

(All these churches were in the vicinity of the present City Hall at that time, but now only Father O'Reilly's Immaculate Conception, Central Presbyterian and Trinity Methodist remain. The others have moved out with the expanding city.)

These churches, some fifty families who refused to be evacuated (some of them northern sympathizers) and some very fine homes that mysteriously escaped the torch and "bushwhackers, robbers and deserters" were what Atlantans found when they began returning, almost before Sherman was out of sight, to begin rebuilding.

Miss Lizzie Perkerson, aunt of Angus Perkerson, who was editor of the Atlanta *Journal-Constitution* magazine for more than forty years, gave a vivid picture of life in the country that winter. In a letter to her brother, Angus, Sr., who was serving in the Confederate Army in Virginia, she wrote of conditions on the farm, which is still standing and is well within the city limits today.

"Pa's place has not got 200 rails [probably fence rails] on it, and not a building of any kind except the house and the old kitchen and the smoke house. We have got one hog, four chickens, two old Yankee mules and ten dogs. . . . All our Negroes are at home and they are the only ones in the neighborhood. You can't imagine how it would take the Yankees down to see a whole gang of old Negroes and children go straggling along. We would tell them to look yonder are some of Sherman's reinforcements."

She reported that the homes of half a dozen of the neighbors were gone. She told of one, a doctor, whose family found a place to move to in South Carolina and started. The second day out he fell off his horse—dead in the road.

"His family buried him by the roadside and went on," Miss Lizzie wrote.

"Cousin Mary and Will's children are at grandma's," she resumed the family news. "The Yankees burned Will's houses and took all the stock. Grandma says indeed she gave one of them three very good licks. He was taking the wheat out of the wheat house and the paddling stick was close by. She just put it to him.

"They all fear I am taking the fever now and I hope not. I feel very badly but I have gone through enough to make a stouter person than me feel badly. I hadn't undressed to go to bed in a month until last night. There had been a great deal of sickness in this country since the army came in here. But I don't think strange of it. The whole country is full of dead horses and mules, and the ditches standing full of stagnate water, enough to kill anything. We have but few soldiers left in these parts now.

"The Yankees broke our loom all to pieces and burned it, but we have just got another one, and if we can get any wool carded we will make you some clothes yet. It is Ma's greatest trouble for fear you are in need and she can't help you."

Back in Atlanta a writer for the *Daily Intelligencer*, which had refugeed to Macon, made a tour of the city and noted in detail the destruction, the roaming packs of half-wild dogs and a strange unearthly stillness.

But like Miss Lizzie, working at her new loom to make cloth to keep the winter cold from her brother fighting in Virginia, this Atlantan's story didn't stop with what was. He went on to what was to be.

"Let us now look to the future!" he wrote in the midst of death and desolation. "That which built Atlanta and made it a flourishing city will again restore it, purified, we trust, in many particulars by the fiery ordeal through which it has passed. Soon the whistles of the steam engines will again be heard . . . soon the cars from Macon and Montgomery and Augusta will bear their burdens into and through our city. Ere long, too, we feel confident that the State Road will be in process of reconstruction. . . . Let no one despond as to the future of our city!"

"We Are Coming to Meet You"

CHAPTER IV

"I attended a funeral once in Pickens County in my State.
. . . It was a poor one-gallus fellow. . . . They buried him in
the midst of a marble quarry; they cut through solid marble
to make his grave; and yet a little tombstone they put above
him was from Vermont. They buried him in the heart of a
pine forest, and yet the pine coffin was imported from Cincinnati. They buried him within touch of an iron mine, and
yet the nails in his coffin and the iron in the shovel that dug
his grave were imported from Pittsburgh. They buried him
by the side of the best sheep-grazing country on earth, and
yet the wool in the coffin bands and the coffin bands themselves were brought from the North. The South didn't furnish
a thing on earth for that funeral but the corpse and the hole
in the ground. . . . They buried him in a New York coat and
a Boston pair of shoes and a pair of breeches from Chicago
and a shirt from Cincinnati, leaving him nothing to carry

into the next world with him to remind him of the country in which he lived, and for which he fought for four years, but the chill of blood in his veins and the marrow in his bones."

Atlantans are extremely fond of that quote. It finds its way into print in one form or another at least once a year. The newspapers and the Chamber of Commerce are especially partial to it and even school children looking for some way of measuring Georgia's business and industrial growth, latch on to it for their essays and term papers with the rapture of prophets stumbling upon fresh truth.

To understand the message's appeal for Atlantans the stranger needs to know about the man who spoke it on a December day twenty-nine years after the Civil War.

He was Henry Woodfin Grady, the ardent young editor of the Atlanta *Constitution* who first wrote and then, blossoming into an orator of renown, spoke of a New South—a region where old enmities were forgotten, where resources in men and land would be expended on something besides those one-crop despots, cotton and tobacco. He preached that economic betterment was the key to all the South's problems and that "waving the bloody shirt" and nursing old hostilities were profitless gestures. He visualized for that New South "her cities vast hives of industry, her countryside the treasures from which their resources are drawn, her streams vocal with whirring spindles."

Mr. Grady came to the *Constitution* by way of the University of Georgia in his native Athens, the University of Virginia and work on two or three other newspapers, including the New York *Herald*. He was but twenty-six years old when he joined the staff of the *Constitution* and in thirteen years he was to become one of the most persuasive writers and speakers in the whole nation. His friend and associate on the paper, Joel Chandler Harris, author of the Uncle Remus stories, was to write of him after his death: "His gift of expression was something marvelous. . . . Above any man I have ever known Mr. Grady possessed the faculty of imparting his personal magnetism to cold type."

Marion J. Verdery, writing for the New York Southern Society, called him "phenomenally gifted," both as a speaker and a writer, adding: "As an orator, he had no equal in the South. He literally mastered his audience regardless of their character, chaining them to the train of his thought and carrying them captive to conviction."

Mr. Grady used these talents to plead constantly for a healing of the breach between the North and the South and to work to bring the three "I's"—investors, industries, immigrants—to the depleted land of his Confederate father, who was killed at Petersburg. Atlanta's four railroads were overtaxed by 1879 and Mr. Grady became fascinated by the prospect of bringing in new railroads. He visited all the railroad centers, made friends with the railroad barons of the day and spent the winter of 1880–81 in New York, writing and trying to interest northern capital in the South.

"I am firmly convinced that as soon as the South is firmly planted on her platform of liberation and progressive development and her position is well understood," he wrote back to the *Constitution*, "we shall see northern capital seeking southern investment with eagerness and the stream of immigration turned toward Georgia."

Mr. Grady's first major and most famous out-of-state speech

was delivered in December 1886 at the banquet of the New England Club in New York. He began with an alleged quote from Senator Ben Hill, some lines which Grady's biographer, Raymond Nixon, later tried to track down and found had been spoken by Hill but were improved immeasurably by Grady himself: "There was a South of slavery and secession— that South is dead. There is a South of union and freedom— that South, thank God, is living, breathing, growing every hour."

That speech, later called the New South speech, established Grady as an orator and as a "great Pacificator," although he was not alone in these endeavors. He was invited back again and again and in 1889 he stood before the Bay State Club of Boston and told the story of the poignant little "one gallus" fellow's funeral in Pickens County.

But only for contrast. For by that time Mr. Grady thought his Southland was well on the way to the new era he had worked for.

"Now we have improved on that," he said, referring to the necessity of importing all the "made" accouterments of the funeral. "We have got the biggest marble-cutting establishment on earth within a hundred yards of that grave. We have got a half-dozen woolen mills right around it, and iron mines, and iron furnaces and iron factories. We are coming to meet you. We are going to take a noble revenge as my friend Mr. Carnegie said last night by invading every inch of your territory with iron, as you invaded ours twenty-nine years ago."

A few days later Henry W. Grady, not quite thirty-nine years old, was dead. He died at home on Peachtree Street December 23, 1889, from pneumonia. His death rocked Georgia and the nation. His friend Andrew Carnegie wired Captain E. P. Howell, publisher of the *Constitution*: "Only those who stood at Mr. Grady's side as we did and heard him at Boston can estimate the extent of the nation's loss in his death."

All over the country, newspapers headlined his death and the florid editorials of the day referred to him as the "apostle of the new faith," the man who "loved a nation back to peace," "an admirable illustration of that sagacious and progressive spirit which is gradually but surely renewing the South."

One of his neighbors and friends in Atlanta reduced the calamity of his death to more personal and intimate terms. "Our city is desolate," said Judge Howard Van Epps the day of the funeral. "We had some great public enterprises in view, that is, Henry had, and we were going to follow him, and overwork him as usual.

"We are disheartened—almost discouraged. Atlanta is so young and fiery, almost fierce in her civic energy and pulls so hard on the reins. Who will drive us now?"

The South as a whole might have needed the spur of Grady's vision and energy, but Atlanta, although missing him, already had the bit in her teeth. She was building, building fast and big.

Already a druggist named John S. Pemberton, who had led cavalry troops under General Joe Wheeler and moved to Atlanta after the war, was puttering around in the backyard with a mixture in a three-legged black iron pot which was to do more for the economy of the nation than Mr. Grady ever dreamed of in his visions of "vast hives of industry." Dr. Pemberton, as he was known, had been calling the stuff "French Wine Cola, the Ideal Nerve and Tonic Stimulant" and more or less dividing his attention between it and a couple of other homemade nostrums, Triplex Liver Pills and Globe Flower Cough Syrup.

The year Mr. Grady was making his New South speech Dr. Pemberton fiddled around some more with his brew, taking out the wine and substituting a pinch of caffeine with the extract of cola.

While he was about it he also changed the name to one which may now be more familiar in some parts of the world than the name of the United Nations or even the United States:

Coca-Cola.

Whether Dr. Pemberton's tonic did anything for the nerves is not known, but a favorite story in Atlanta is that it was very efficacious as a hangover cure and a queasy-stomach soother.

Asa Griggs Candler, who had come to town with $1.75 in his pocket and taken a job at another drugstore, was too good a Methodist and too frugal to have hangovers. But he did have an uneasy stomach and he found Dr. Pemberton's brew so helpful he bought the formula for two thousand dollars in 1891. Meanwhile, somebody had discovered by happy accident that a teaspoonful of the syrup mixed with charged water, instead of plain water, was a zippy drink and Mr. Candler decided to take it out of the medicinal class and start peddling it as a drink for pleasure.

Local lore is full of accounts of how the Candler boys enraged the tenants beneath them in a building on Decatur Street by forgetting to watch the source of the family fortune—the Coca-Cola syrup kettle—and letting the sticky brown liquid boil over and run downstairs. Whether this is true or not the boys watched their papa's two thousand dollar recipe boil into an asset which in 1919 while the old man was busy serving as Mayor of Atlanta, they and other relatives sold for $25 million. (Mr. Asa Candler, Sr., did retain for himself one percent of his Coca-Cola stock.)

One of the three banks handling the transaction was local, the small Trust Company of Georgia, now known the world over as "the Coca-Cola bank." Ernest Woodruff was president of the Trust Company and that is how his son, Robert, happened to give up the trucking business and become immersed in the soft drink business. Today Robert Woodruff, sometimes called one of the richest men in the world, is estimated to be worth between $75 and $100 million.

Meanwhile, the amber fluid which Atlantans regard with almost patriotic affection, has trickled fortunes in all directions.

Mr. Candler sold the first bottling rights to a couple of lawyers from Chattanooga for one dollar, which he didn't bother to collect. From this bottling franchise and others subsequently sold, numbering more than a thousand in the United States, multitudes of people have grown very wealthy. Schools and hospitals and libraries have been endowed. Side industries have sprung up for the manufacture of bottles, coolers and crates. And the advertising industry alone has received a tremendous boost from the example of this, the most heavily advertised single commodity in the United States.

The Coca-Cola Company has offices elsewhere, but the main office is still an old-fashioned-looking building at 310 North Avenue—as fascinating to Atlanta children when they pass it on their way to the Varsity or the Yellow Jacket to get a hot dog as Ali Baba's cave. For one thing, it's well known that visitors can drink all the free Cokes they want in that building. And then it is said to hold somewhere in its secret vitals that most golden of all golden geese—the formula for making Coca-Cola.

Mr. Woodruff, too, has other homes—one in New York and a plantation in South Georgia, which has been frequented by such famous quail hunters as ex-President Eisenhower. But his main establishment and those of some of his brother Coca-Cola millionaires is on West Pace's Ferry Road—sometimes called "Coca-Cola Row."

The style of architecture?

I'm not sure, but local wags call it "roccocola."

Sherman had barely got out of town and Henry W. Grady had not even arrived when another famous Atlanta business was started. Morris Rich, a small South Georgia merchant, borrowed five hundred dollars from his brother, William, in 1867 and opened a small retail dry goods store on Whitehall Street—very like one of those buildings you might remember from *Gone With the Wind*, a rough pine rectangle measuring a scant twenty by seventy-five feet.

According to store records Rich's did five thousand dollars' worth of business that year and had five employees. In 1962 Rich's did $95 million worth of business and the other day Richard H. Rich, grandson of the founder and chairman of the board, estimated that the store would pass the $100 million mark in 1963. For people who are knowledgeable about department-store figures, that means that M. Rich's little postwar enterprise has outstripped all other stores south of New York, including those in Philadelphia, Baltimore and Washington, and the fabled Nieman-Marcus in Dallas is scarcely in the running. It now has forty-five hundred employees, not counting the thousand who join the force at Christmas time, and that rough little pine cubicle on Whitehall Street has been replaced by two blocks of stores downtown and three branch stores in the suburbs.

The figures are impressive and Atlantans, when they occasionally bump into them on the business page of the newspapers, are pleased and proud, of course.

"You always like to see *nice* people do well," an elderly customer of Rich's remarked.

Actually it is the "niceness" of Rich's and not the scope of the big old store's financial success which has enshrined it in the hearts of Atlantans in a position roughly between motherhood and pure drinking water. Rich's calls itself an Atlanta institution and it is all of that—one of the last family-run enterprises of its kind in the country, with all the neighborliness and personal involvement in the community that the words "family-run" imply.

Not long ago I had to call the police station on a story and I dialed Rich's by mistake. When the store operator answered I said clumsily, "Oh, I'm sorry—I wanted the police."

Instead of curtly disconnecting me—as the operator of a local coal company does when she gets a call intended for Grady Hospital—the Rich's operator said with swift concern, "Honey, are you in trouble? You want me to get the police for you?"

I wasn't in trouble and I didn't need her to get the police for me but, like many another Atlantan, I am certain that if I were and if I did, it would be perfectly logical to call Rich's. You can take practically any problem to Rich's, get just about anything you need there, *including* the police.

Back in the great depression of the 1930s, Atlanta's school system found itself without money and was paying off the teachers with scrip. Walter Rich, nephew of Morris and cousin of Dick Rich, sent word to the authorities that Rich's still had cash in the till and the teachers could swap their scrip for it—no obligation. Hundreds of teachers and ex-teachers remember that gesture with gratitude and to all Atlanta it stands as proof of a special, we're-in-this-thing-together attitude at Rich's. The city later redeemed $645,000 in scrip from Rich's.

On Labor Day weekend in 1945 troops were being moved out from Fort McPherson and the post's safes were time-locked until Tuesday. Somebody called Rich's and the store advanced the money the Army needed. The tragedy of the Winecoff Hotel fire in 1946 reached far outside Atlanta to the families of 109 people who died in it and to many others who were badly injured. Relatives of the victims poured into town, bewildered and grief-stricken, to claim their bodies and to try to make funeral arrangements. Representatives of Rich's went out to help them and the shrouds needed were given—as a token of profound sympathy.

Rich's has long served as Atlanta's "Saturday bank," cashing thousands of checks all day long. Its credit policies are so liberal it's a poor citizen indeed who doesn't have a charge account there.

A young woman I know married a widower with a house full of small children and his financial affairs in a real mess due to illness and business reverses.

"The first thing we're going to do," she announced firmly, "is restore his credit at Rich's. He needs that for his self-respect."

The inference is that with Rich's for you, who can be against you? Needless to say, Rich's has fostered this notion so skillfully that even shoplifters expect to be treated tenderly there. An old lady who was hauled up short by the store security squad, her reticule bulging with pilfered jewelry, gloves and silverware, was outraged when she related the experience to a city detective.

"I've been getting things at Rich's for fifty years," she said aggrievedly, "and this is the first time they ever hurt my feelings."

Rich's return and exchange policy is so famous that department stores over the country have sent envoys to study it. The word in Atlanta is that no matter where you bought it, they'll take it back at Rich's. Naturally this policy has been exploited to the hilt by a few con artists but oddly enough Rich's does not feel that it has suffered. They have figures to show that the percentages of returns and exchanges runs about twice as high as the national average for such things and the store officials actually seem pleased about it. Even the Chamber of Commerce relates the story of the woman who bought a cake for her daughter's wedding at Rich's and after it was eaten complained that the layers under the icing had been yellow instead of white. The fact that Rich's gave her another cake—a white one—always struck me as singularly soft-headed. But recently I saw the wisdom of it.

The aunt of a friend of mine, visiting Atlanta from New Orleans, returned to Rich's a pair of shoes bought at Holmes —and was so delighted with her coup she lingered long enough to buy her entire summer wardrobe and her next winter's coat.

Some time afterward I related this to Mr. Rich as an ex-

ample of how the store outfoxes the foxy, but he seemed
vaguely distressed by that interpretation. Rich's didn't refund
the money on the Holmes shoes from any such crass commercial motive, he assured me earnestly.

"We merely wanted to be of service to the lady," he said.

The service of Rich's to the community is indisputable. In
1943 the Rich's Foundation was formed for the purpose of distributing some of the big store's profits where they would do
the most good. Recipients have included the Emory School
of Business Administration, an outpatient clinic at Georgia
Baptist Hospital, a grant to St. Joseph's Infirmary, a lab for
the industrial engineering department at Georgia Tech, an
electronic computer center at Tech, and radio station
WABE-FM for the city and county school systems.

Frank Neely, a nonfamily power at Rich's since 1924 when
Walter Rich brought him from a textile mill, whence he had
gone from Georgia Tech, to apply his skills to the operation of
the store, rose to the post of president, chairman of the board
and now chairman of the executive committee. He and the
Riches have always been leaders in community affairs, and so
have most of the executives, major or minor. This, too, is
company policy.

"We tell our people we want them to do *something* for
Atlanta," Dick Rich says. "We don't care what it is—church
work, the Red Cross, the PTA, anything they want—but service beyond personal gain and one's workaday concerns is, after
all, the obligation of the citizen."

For himself Mr. Rich feels that his efforts for the public
weal are merely in the Atlanta tradition. There are cities, he
knows, where business and industrial leaders insulate themselves against the concerns of city government and grubby

social problems. Political corruption flourishes in such places and, more recently, racial strife.

Atlanta business leaders have a long-standing habit of making themselves available to the Mayor when he needs counsel and now that they have a hand in electing a Governor they are likewise available to him.

Atlanta has many other department stores and specialty shops, some of them mighty elegant and almost as imaginative as Rich's. The nearest runner-up in size and scope of community activity is the handsome Peachtree Street emporium, Davison-Paxon, established in Atlanta in 1897 and affiliated with the Macy chain in 1927. The original owners were well-known Atlantans, and Davison's counts the new owners as of Georgian origin since the descendants of Lazarus Straus of Talbotton, Georgia, founded Macy's.

When Davison's moved off Whitehall Street to its present location, prophets of doom said they were going "too far uptown." The town not only followed but moved so far and so fast that Davison's, along with many other stores, had to build a branch at Lenox Square out Peachtree Road. It also has branches in Athens, Macon, Augusta, Columbus, Columbia (South Carolina) and a smart little beach shop on Sea Island.

This last one is notable to me because some years back I was assigned to cover the visit of Queen Juliana of the Netherlands to the Georgia coast. Since the queen was very shy and retiring, reporters saw little of her. Finally, hearing that the queen had left her suite and was loose on the hotel grounds, I started looking for her. She was in Davison's beach shop buying bathing suits—Size 48.

As a transportation and communication center Atlanta first attracted businessmen with something to distribute. They shipped their goods in here to be relayed to all points of the southeast. Warehouses came next and then regional offices and eventually plants. By 1961, Virgil Hartley was writing in the *Atlanta Magazine*: "Manufacturing has overtaken that giant, transportation, and is now the single largest employer in the Atlanta area."

Lockheed's plant near Marietta—the largest aircraft plant in the United States under one roof—is the biggest employer in the state, with jobs for 14,500 people and a payroll which over a period of ten years runs into $748 million. This plant came to Atlanta in the World War II years as Bell Aircraft, known locally as "the bummer plant."

General Motors Corporation is another big manufacturer and another big employer, going back to 1927 when the corporation decided to decentralize its production facilities in Detroit. Ford came to town in 1915 and by 1960 had ceremoniously rolled its millionth car off the assembly line in Hapeville.

These are representative of the many northern concerns which started moving south even before the ashes had cooled. There are others that are native or near-native and distinctively Atlanta.

Scripto, for instance.

Atlantans have a certain proprietary pride in this comparatively young and modest member of the highly competitive mechanical pencil and ball pen industry. For one thing, it is headed by James V. Carmichael, an enormously popular native son who ran for Governor in 1946, collecting the highest number of popular votes ever cast for a candidate in Georgia, but losing to the county unit system and Gene Talmadge.

Mr. Carmichael, called Jimmy by great numbers of Georgians, although he has attained the dignity of his early fifties and has a touch of gray at the temples, was instrumental in bringing the Bell Bomber Plant to Marietta. Starting as its legal counsel, he became vice-president and general manager. After the war he was invited to join Scripto as an assistant to the president, M. A. Ferst, who founded the firm in 1923.

"I didn't know anything about making pens and pencils," Mr. Carmichael recalls, "but I agreed to try it for a few months and if I found or they found I wasn't suited for the job, I was going back to the practice of law."

So well suited was young Jimmy Carmichael to this business that he moved up to the post of president when Mr. Ferst retired from active management to serve as chairman of the board. Today Scripto's main plant in Atlanta has branched out to major production facilities in Toronto, London, Mexico City and the countries of Southern Rhodesia, New Zealand and Australia.

Sales reached a towering $25 million in 1962 with people in a hundred different nations buying the bright, inexpensive pens and pencils and recently added lighters.

A thing about Scripto that Atlantans now take for granted but which has interested the national press in recent years is its employment of Negroes. Of thirteen hundred employees, eight hundred and fifty are Negro women, most of them uneducated and unskilled when they started but so adept at their jobs that some have stayed on as long as forty years. By now, second and even third generations are coming to the plant. As pleased as they are to have these, Scripto officials are doubly proud that the first Negro accepted for the Naval Academy was the son of a Scripto employee.

Mr. Carmichael demonstrated his interest in public affairs by running for Governor, although he has little personal taste for politics, and he has continued to devote energy, enthusiasm and great chunks of time to community betterment. The work of the Atlanta Art Association, of which he is president, is personally satisfying to him for aesthetic and, surprisingly enough, economic reasons.

"When people are poor, as we were right after the war," he points out, "they have to devote their energies to scrabbling for food. My grandparents lived during Reconstruction Days and they had their hands full trying to wrest a living from the land. When things ease up a little the next thing people strive for is education for their children and an improvement in health conditions. And after that, if they've worked hard and succeeded a little, they have some time and a few extra dollars they can spend for things that give them pleasure—a little beauty in their lives, pictures maybe, music."

Although there have always been individuals who could afford these things, as a city Atlanta has only recently attained that measure of security and leisure. And according to Mr. Carmichael it's high time, for purely practical considerations, if nothing else.

"Our industries are bringing in technical people, engineers, executives, all with good educational backgrounds. They want advantages for their children—museums, a symphony orchestra, concerts, the theater. Unless the community provides such things these people are not going to stay. They are an economic necessity."

1   Hurt Park taken over for a spring party by students.

2   The lighting of the great tree on Thanksgiving night is a community tradition.

3   A trash man makes a pickup under the viaduct.

4   Atlanta's favorite kind of home.

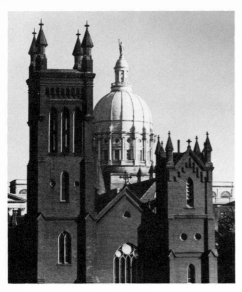

5   The Capitol dome framed by the
oldest church in Atlanta, the
Church of the Immaculate Conception.

6   On the way to the wash hole for a summer baptizing.

This is one business leader's personal community crusade. Others have other projects. And if Henry W. Grady should happen to be watching from some celestial lookout he must be pleased that his "young and fiery" city conquers one problem and promptly sets for itself another.

The question Judge Van Epps asked the day of Grady's funeral, "Who will drive us now?" has found an answer: Practically everybody.

They're Counting Our Votes.

CHAPTER V

Atlantans, being Georgians and therefore mostly southern and largely country, love politics. This may go back to the pre-television, pre-automobile days when there wasn't much excitement in the boondocks and branch heads except that generated by the exercise of men striving for public office. If there had been anywhere else to go, any other form of public entertainment, it's possible the rural southerner wouldn't have developed such a marked taste for oratory and barbecue.

Having little enough to divert them, however, at "lay-by time," when there was nothing to do in the fields except let the crops grow, and the summer protracted meeting had run its course, a political rally at the county seat was a welcome event. Men of all ages from bearded grandpas to shirt-tail boys saddled up horses, hitched the mule to the wagon or set out afoot to hear such spellbinders as fiery old Bob Toombs,

Little Aleck Stephens, Tom Watson and, in later years, Ol'
Gene Talmadge.

Even before they had the right to vote the womenfolks
frequently went along too, listening from the sidelines, mind-
ing the children, watching the hickory smoke curl up from the
pits where a beef and several shoats roasted, laved in sauce
and man-tended.

You have but to read some of the old speeches to realize
that politics in Georgia for many generations was better than
any road show. Tom Watson's "ideal goddess"—Eloquence—
was everybody's. The conduct of public affairs evolved from a
game that gentlemen played in the days of the Revolution
to a game anybody could play and the talented or lucky amateur frequently won.

Atlanta, which wrested the state capitol from Milledgeville
in 1868, has held for nearly a hundred years a strangely paradoxical position in state politics. It has offered the arena for
the main events of the show.

Here is the State House, its gold dome visible from all
directions, dominating, when the sun hits it, even a skyline
of towering office buildings. (The gold for the dome was
brought to town by wagon train in 1958 by the people of
Dahlonega, the little town in the hill country where America's
first gold rush was staged and the first U. S. Mint operated.
The mint was abandoned many years ago but people still pan
for gold and nearly every family had gold dust or nuggets to
give for gilding the capitol dome.)

Here the General Assembly convenes, turning the town
for forty days and nights into a churning, roiling cauldron of
political activity—a watched pot. The hotels burgeon with
senators and representatives from the 159 counties; traffic

around Capitol Square is swelled by their cars. Restaurant and nightclub business booms. For a time it seems that every third man on the street is either in politics or wants to be in politics.

In election years the state campaign headquarters come to town and Peachtree Street takes on a carnival air with the banners of the candidates flapping in the breeze and sound-truck pitchmen roaming at large.

For his tenure of office Atlanta is the Governor's home. Until 1921 the executive mansion was on downtown Peach-tree Street—a turreted Victorian, iron-fenced relic which the state replaced with the present Henry Grady Hotel in 1924, moving the Governor to a gloomy granite architectural hor-ror in Ansley Park. (The 1962 legislature launched plans to replace that by acquiring the West Pace's Ferry Road estate of former Atlanta mayor Robert F. Maddox as the site for a new $25 million appropriately colonial Governor's Mansion.)

The presence of the state's First Family in Atlanta gives the populace a certain proprietary feeling about them. The lighting of the Christmas lights on the lawn and rooftop of the old mansion in Ansley Park is an annual fete which draws lines of automobiles, loaded with children, to the Prado. State functions and state visitors at the big gray granite pile on the hill keep life interesting for the neighbors. And occasionally something like an effigy burning or a student demonstration on the lawn makes the nights lively.

In Governor Marvin Griffin's regime the neighbors turned out in their pajamas to watch Georgia Tech students burn the Governor in effigy in protest to his ruling that Tech couldn't play a football team with a Negro on it.

Some neighbors still speak with amusement of the way

the moving vans plied up and down like busy little tugboats
before the Governor's Mansion in 1947. That was the year
when Georgia had two Governors at once—Herman Talmadge, now Senator Talmadge, contending by virtue of a
write-in vote to be the heir apparent of his father, Ol' Gene,
who was elected and died before he could take office, and
M. E. Thompson, the Lieutenant-Governor who held (and
was subsequently sustained by the State Supreme Court)
that the right of succession was his. Ellis Arnall, the out-
going Governor, tried to hang on until the courts settled the
issue and between the three of them moving in and moving
out, the turnover at the mansion was something to see.

That's Atlanta, the capital city and the main arena for
the state political show.

But there's the other side—the Atlanta, which has, politi-
cally, been in the position of the well-known illegitimate
child at the family reunion from the 1880s to the stirring
1960s.

A unique arrangement of vote counting called the county
unit system was responsible for this.

For generations, students of government have been coming to Georgia to behold democracy's anathema, election
by the few, treated locally as a sacred tribal rite.

Professor Albert B. Saye of the University of Georgia called
it "the most distinctive feature of Georgia's political system."
A study by the University of Virginia noted it resulted in
making Atlanta "the most disfranchised city in America."

The county unit system was born of the conviction that
electing state officials and representatives in the U. S. Congress by popular vote would put political control in the hands
of what Tom Watson called "a few city bosses . . . using

corporation influence, the job-lash, money, whiskey and log-rolling." The rural counties were where virtue and honor resided, Watson and many of his successors firmly believed.

From the 1880s to 1917 the system existed informally, urgently defended and upheld by people like Watson. In 1917 with the enactment of the Neill Primary Act it became law —a system whereby all candidates for Congress, Governor, State House officials and justices of the State Supreme Court and Court of Appeals were elected according to the number of counties they carried and not the number of votes they received. A candidate receiving the highest number of popular votes in a county was considered to have carried the county and to be entitled to the full vote of such county. The weight of that county's influence was measured on a unit basis, two votes for each representative it had in the Lower House of the General Assembly.

Under that system the smallest county in the state, little Echols in South Georgia, with a population of 1876 people, had one unit representing 938 voters. Fulton County (Atlanta) with a population of 556,326, had six units, representing 24,183 voters.

Naturally the people of the cities, most of whom had come from the country originally, railed out against this disfranchisement, but it wasn't until 1962 that they had any real hope. When the U. S. Supreme Court ruled early in 1962 that the Federal District Court had power to grant a group of Nashville citizens more representation in the legislature, Georgia politicians—wrote *Constitution* political editor Reg Murphy—"knew the jig was up."

Governor Ernest Vandiver called the legislature back into special session in the spring of 1962 in a bit of window dressing which was supposed to show the rural areas the politicals still were fighting for them. But Vandiver and the legislature both knew well enough that they could not be successful.

While the legislature sat through the twelfth day of that grim special session, a three-judge Federal Court sitting half a mile away in the third-floor courtroom of Atlanta's Old Post Office Building, began tearing into the system.

The legislature made minor concessions—a few more units for the cities. The courts said it wasn't enough. The State Democratic leadership decided any further granting of units to cities was impossible. The Democratic Executive Committee met and decided to hold the first popular-vote elections in about fifty years.

Ex-Governor Marvin Griffin, making a bid for a comeback, panicked. He asked the committee to hold the election on a plurality basis, figuring a split vote would help him if there was no runoff.

The committee, dominated by the outgoing Governor S. Ernest Vandiver, wouldn't have it. It said there must be a majority vote. Griffin's chances ended with that decision, but it wouldn't be proved until the hot summer's campaign was over and the votes were in on September 12. Griffin, a tough old veteran of the "hog-and-hominy" school of politics, and an arch-segregationist, was defeated by Carl Sanders, a young Augusta lawyer called a moderate by his supporters. (Sanders said of himself, "I'm a segregationist, but not a damned fool.")

The attacks on the county unit system continued. The legislature was pushed into another corner by a three-judge Federal Court decision during the summer, saying there must be reapportionment. The General Assembly came back into session in late September and boosted the Atlanta metropolitan area's representation in the 1963 Senate from one to twelve senators.

This brought on another election in a summer so election-ridden that people joked they couldn't go home to dinner any day until they had dropped by the polls and voted.

Everybody got into that race for the Senate—old-timers in city and county jobs who hadn't dared to aspire to the state senate as long as there was only one seat, fresh young lawyers, housewives, Negroes and Republicans. When the smoke of battle cleared, Atlanta hadn't elected any women (one came close) but it had included in the round dozen the first Negro since the turn of the century, a lawyer named Leroy Johnson, and a white Republican, an insurance man named Dan MacIntyre, III.

For the first time in its history the capital city has a respectable place at the council table in state leadership. The voices of the old-guard rural politicians, viewing with alarm the political domination of "that silk stocking crowd at the Capital City Club," are still heard but they're growing fainter.

Actually, the rural resident has more chance of seeing the influence of Atlanta's "silk stocking crowd" than of the corrupt big-city bosses Tom Watson feared. Atlanta businessmen have historically taken an interest in government. One of the more famous instances was Coca-Cola magnate Asa Candler, who took office as mayor in 1917 to save the city from bankruptcy. He not only declined to take any salary for his services but he lent the city money from his private fortune to pull it out of the red.

Mills B. Lane, the colorful president of the far-flung Citizens and Southern National Bank chain, sent out postcards to sound out the electorate on the candidacy of another businessman, Ivan Allen, Jr., before the Mayor's race in 1961. The town was going to be hard-pressed to find a successor to Bill Hartsfield, a man acceptable to business interests and at the same time dynamic and colorful enough to capture the imagination of the random voter.

Allen, a well-to-do second generation Atlanta office supply company executive, silver-haired, fifty years old, showed up well in Banker Lane's poll, and he entered the race with the blessings of the Chamber of Commerce vote, Atlanta newspapers and a chunk of the so-called liberal and Negro vote. It was a five-man race and it wasn't easy.

Three of the contenders were old pros who had seen service in the legislature, the county commission or both. The fourth, like Allen, was an amateur, but what an amateur. Lester Garfield Maddox, forty-five, operator of a fried-chicken emporium called the Pickrick, running on a segregation ticket with the support of White Citizens Council groups and, many supposed, the Ku Klux Klan, had all the color formerly associated with the old-school country politician.

He was sharp and feisty and funny but also alarming to a largely educated electorate, bent on economic and cultural progress. When he yelled that the election of Allen would mean that Auburn Avenue, the main Negro business district, "will run your city," voters raised up in the Hartsfield tradition, shuddered.

In the end, after a full summer of campaigning, a primary and a runoff, Allen swept to a decisive victory over Maddox.

Bill Hartsfield, the old campaigner, took over the microphone in the *Constitution* newsroom, where the returns were being tabulated and radio and television crews recorded the results, to praise Atlantans for once more choosing wisely.

For as long as he lives, of course, Hartsfield will be "Mister Mayor" to many Atlantans. He held the nation's record for service as a Mayor—more than a quarter of a century—and he has been named in many polls as one of the country's top municipal chieftains from the standpoint of achievement.

Caustic, witty, full of fight, it was characteristic of Mayor Bill that when he retired in 1961 he didn't sag down in a rocking chair or on a park bench somewhere and settle for being the city's elder statesman. He got himself a new wife, a new job, a new home—and he joined the PTA!

Some Atlantans tut-tutted when he filed suit for divorce from the first Mrs. Hartsfield, a shy, retiring woman who had been practically invisible to the public the thirty-two years of their marriage. Some of his contemporaries chuckled appreciatively that at the age of seventy-one he was eligible for the PTA. (The second Mrs. Hartsfield was a widow with a little boy.)

Come to think about it, his first PTA meeting could even symbolize something.

His successor, the new Mayor Allen, happened to be on the program. Although a man of social poise, Mayor Allen had not yet acquired Hartsfield's expertise as a welcomer, an opener, a ribbon-cutter and a shovel-handler at civic occasions. He stood up on the stage at R. L. Hope School and said he was "glad to be here at E. Rivers School."

Laughing but flustered herself, the principal said warmly, "Thank you, Mayor Hartsfield!"

I interviewed Mayor Hartsfield a couple of weeks before he went out of office and found him unable to keep his mind on

reminiscences. Looking back doesn't interest him half as
much as looking ahead. Besides, some of his recollections
caused his adrenalin to flow so freely he would be caught
midway in a story and leap nimbly from his chair and give a
blistering, devastatingly funny imitation of a detractor, a foot-
dragger or an all-out opponent to some of his civic innova-
tions.

Once Hartsfield was defeated—by a real-estate insurance
man named Roy LeCraw and a margin of 111 votes in 1940.
LeCraw served but fourteen months when the United States
entered World War II and he was recalled to active duty with
the National Guard, in which he was a major. Hartsfield re-
claimed the office with a sweeping victory over a field of seven
other candidates.

But he learned something from that defeat.

"I thought I did such a helluva good job I didn't need to
campaign," he said. "But that's not right. You've got to fight
every time! You could pave the streets with gold, reduce taxes
to a nickel a year and scent the sewers with Chanel No. 5
and they wouldn't remember you unless you reminded
them!"

Even on the eve of quitting office the Mayor was ready with
a roster of projects he passionately believes are for the betterment of Atlanta. A long-time fighter, both in the courts and
out, against the county unit system, he noted its death with
satisfaction but, typically, didn't spend much time dwelling
on it. He wants to see the city limits expanded again. Getting
them pushed out from 37 to 118 miles was a major battle in
1952. He thinks some new form of taxes must be found to
spread the burden of the central city operation to the shoul-

ders of people who work and earn a living in it but who, poor
benighted souls, live somewhere outside the city limits.

"The Atlanta image," as Hartsfield called it, is of intense,
urgent, personal importance to him.

"A city must have pride," he said. "It must believe in itself. If you're all the time talking poor you *look* poor.
There's such a thing as civic hypochondria."

Talking poor isn't one of Atlanta's besetting sins. It has
been accused of the opposite, and the weight swung by
money was duly noted by one of the candidates who was
not supported by Banker Mills B. Lane the summer Allen was
elected.

There was danger, predicted this orator, that if Allen won,
the people of Atlanta would "change the name of Peachtree
Street to *Mills Lane!*"

Although Hartsfield valued the voter, as only the successful
politician can, he never let the desire for votes obscure his
vision or dull the edge of his tongue when he felt the occasion warranted it.

There's a now-famous story of the time some movie press
agents brought a trick horse into his office to receive the official welcome. The Mayor hadn't known the welcome involved anything but a photograph and perhaps a pat on the
nose for the horse but when the press agent asked him to say
a few words, he was by no means speechless.

"This is an historic occasion," he began with a fine roll of
rhetoric. "It is the first time I've had the pleasure of receiving in my office a *whole* horse!"

The Darker Third

The talent for being surprised and gratified at themselves is nothing new to Atlantans. We have in us a large streak of the beldame who asked with classic self-astonishment, "La, me, can this be I?" We see ourselves as a plain and sturdy hen perpetually hatching ducklings.

But the part of our town that perhaps evokes the most amazement in the most people is the one-third usually referred to as "ouah Nigra community."

Atlantans mean to say "Negro," they really do. And some of them manage it quite nicely without even the slightest pause, without even the faintest flush of self-consciousness, before pronouncing the word. Many more say it carefully, too conscientiously, usually overworking it around the Negro friends who approve it and dropping it altogether the rest of the time. The reason for this is simple. Most Georgians now grown were reared to believe that no well-brought-up white

person ever referred to members of the Other Race as anything but "colored." "Nigger" was absolutely taboo, the language of the po' white. "Nigra" was more dignified and altogether nicer but likely, for some mysterious reason nobody
ever explained, to hurt the feelings of the colored person.

So the gently bred, those with an innate considerateness,
never admitted Negro to their vocabularies. The fact that it
is the name of the race and correctly and proudly used by
members of that race, has shaken our habit of speech con-
siderably but has by no means dislodged it.

So we refer to "ouah Nigra community" and although the
accent may be archaic and the entire term a shade discredit-
able, it is no less true.

There have been dramatic, spine-tingling changes in recent
years, of course. The old patterns of segregation have shifted,
laws separating the races have crumbled. Led by the newspapers and pushed by William B. Hartsfield, the man who
was their Mayor from 1937 to 1961, Atlantans first timorously
then out of stubborn practicality and finally proudly, took the
lead in Georgia, if not the whole South, in admitting Negroes
to proper citizenship.

Six years before the Supreme Court's historic 1954 decision
Atlanta began quietly hiring Negro policemen. We have had
a Negro member of the Board of Education since 1953. Municipal golf courses were desegregated in 1955, followed by
trolleys and all branches of the Public Library in 1959 and
the new jet airport in 1960. The stirring saga of school desegregation in 1961 and the subsequent falling of racial bar-
riers at department store lunch counters, movie theaters and
the opera is told elsewhere. The election of an Atlanta Negro

to the state senate in the summer of 1962—the first member
of his race to serve in that body since Reconstruction Days—
is the very symbol of an undreamed of (by most white people anyhow) political and social revolution in the South. Negro doctors practice at Grady Hospital and have been admitted
to membership in the Fulton County Medical Society.

Even so, Atlanta's Negro citizens, as of this year 1963, still
live in a very nearly separate world from her white citizens.
It may be generations before the two worlds ever truly meet
and merge.

And while this separation exists the wonder grows. Those
white Atlantans whose acquaintance with Negroes is limited
to a faithful maid or laundress, an elevator man or a yard man,
are eternally astonished by the tales of the affluent and elegant and richly intellectual life which is lived by certain Negro
citizens in an area vaguely linked with Atlanta University,
somewhere south of town.

Poppy Cannon's account in A Gentle Knight of her marriage to Walter White, the white-skinned Atlanta Negro who
became executive secretary of the National Association for
the Advancement of Colored People, contains a description
of social life in Atlanta which had an Arabian Nights quality
for many southern white readers. She wrote of the great
homes, the country estates, the receptions and the teas and
cocktail parties, the art collections, the superb cookery and in
general the taste and intelligence she encountered among Atlanta's first Negro families. (A "first" Negro family is usually
one that sprang into prominence during the Reconstruction
Days or one whose head was a public official, as in the case of
B. A. Rucker, revenue collector in the thirteen years from the
McKinley to the Taft administrations.)

Not many white Atlantans dreamed that this world existed, although perhaps more are now acquainted with it than most of their neighbors suppose. A wealthy Negro leader told me that he and his wife exchange dinner invitations with about fifty white Atlanta couples. He carefully refrained from identifying them, probably to protect them from the wrath of such militant white supremacy groups as the White Citizens Council, but he said they are for the most part southern-born people whose professional interests coincide with his and provide an area of compatibility having nothing to do with race.

Except for these relatively rare excursions by the venturesome few, however, white Atlantans and Negro Atlantans go their separate ways. The Negro community, numbering 185,000 persons, or approximately one-third of the population, has its commercial center in Auburn Avenue—known locally as "Sweet Auburn"—said to be the richest Negro street in the world.

It's not an impressive street, being given over largely to small, dingy-looking buildings housing Negro barbershops, grocery stores and an occasional restaurant or beer parlor. But sandwiched among these lesser enterprises is the Atlanta Life Insurance Company, whose $40 million in assets qualifies it as the largest Negro stock company in the world. Here is also the Citizens Trust Company with assets of $7 million, the only Negro bank to belong to the Federal Reserve System; the Atlanta World, one of the few Negro daily newspapers in the country; and the Mutual Federal Savings and Loan Association of Atlanta with assets of $11 million, the biggest institution of its kind in the South.

The "Sweet Auburn" Avenue building which houses the Atlanta Life Insurance Company, among other Negro offices, is the Herndon Building. It bears the name of a man who is one of Atlanta's favorite success stories—Alonzo Herndon, slave and farmhand turned barber.

Born at Social Circle, Georgia, Alonzo Herndon moved to Senoia and started cutting hair when freedom came.

"He had no shop or adequate tools," related M. S. Stuart in his volume on Negro business, *Economic Detour*. "But in some way he picked up an old pair of scissors and an old-fashioned razor on which with a whetstone and a little water he always kept the finest edge. He rented a little corner in the colored section and soon his reputation as a fine barber spread throughout the community. In a short time he had to work until midnight every Saturday to serve his patrons."

After three months in Senoia, Mr. Herndon saved enough money to open his own barbershop in Jonesboro and in 1882 at the age of twenty-four he made his way to Atlanta and found a job as a journeyman barber. Four years later he was able to open his own shop on Whitehall Street where he won such a following among his white customers that the proprietors of the Markham House, the then new and richly appointed hotel, persuaded him to run the hotel barbershop.

The hotel was destroyed by fire in 1896, but by that time Mr. Herndon was ready to branch out on his own. He had saved his money and he used some of it to travel—always on a mission, to inspect the finest barbershops in the world. He journeyed to New Orleans and Los Angeles and San Francisco, picking up ideas wherever he went and when he came back to Atlanta he was ready to open on Peachtree Street the most elegant barbershop in the country, from its crystal chandeliers to its brass spittoons.

"Here was a colored man," wrote Stuart, "daring to make a

determined fight for white business against white competitors. Many said it was a foolhardy venture, but soon in his three shops he was giving employment to seventy-five men."

From barbering Mr. Herndon turned his attention to insurance, launching with a couple of secondhand desks, one typewriter and a few rusty pen staffs the business which was to become Atlanta Life Insurance Company. He married the former Adrienne McNeal, a successful Negro actress, and built at 1 University Place a cream brick mansion as a monument to his progress. The distance he traveled from slavery to the position as master in his own white columned "great house" is depicted in a mural which Mr. Herndon had painted in the house itself.

Today his son, Norris B. Herndon, who was graduated from Atlanta University and Harvard School of Business Administration, heads the insurance company and lives in the columned mansion. He is one of the Big Four in Negro financial circles. (The other three are Clayton R. Yates, real estate developer and co-owner of the Yates and Milton drugstore chain; Lorimer D. Milton, president of the Citizens Trust Company and partner in the drug concern; and Jessie B. Blayton, president of the Mutual Federal and owner of the Negro radio station WERD.)

Mr. Herndon died in 1927, leaving behind, in addition to his home, Herndon Building and insurance business, one of his barbershops—the Herndon Shop at 68 Broad Street. The shop, in the heart of the white business section, still caters to white trade and many an old-school Atlanta gentleman feels it necessary to "introduce" a newcomer before he can be properly received at Herndon's.

Although Auburn Avenue is the physical center of Negro

commerce, its true center is a cluster of variegated brick build-
ings on a tree-shaded campus on a hill overlooking downtown
Atlanta. Atlanta University, with its five associate institutions
—Morris Brown, Morehouse, Clark and Spelman Colleges and
Gammon Theological Seminary—is both the center of our
Darker Third's social and intellectual life and the lodestar of
its economy.

The University Center, the biggest Negro educational center in the country, has drawn gifted people to the area, frequently as students and teachers, and has nurtured and sustained, sheltered and refreshed them in what might otherwise
have been an onerous segregated society.

Walter Akin is an example. Mr. Akin is known to older
sportswriters as "Chief" Akin—a Negro Indian chief no less.
He was given the title by his red-skinned team mates at Virginia's Hampton Institute where before World War I he ex-
celled as a football, baseball, basketball and track star. A native of Delaware, Mr. Akin came to Georgia when he returned
from France after World War I, because of Lucy Rucker,
daughter of the aforementioned Atlanta "First Family." He
and Miss Rucker (whose maternal grandfather, incidentally,
was the Reconstruction Days Negro Congressman Jefferson
Long of Macon) met and were married in Macon. They came
to Atlanta and he took a job as football coach at Atlanta University, simultaneously launching his highly successful construction business.

Today one of the richest men in Atlanta, black or white,
"Chief" Akin in semiretirement presides over a real estate
empire which includes the 129-unit ultramodern Waluhaje
Apartments (so called for the first two letters in his family's
first names—Walter, Lucy, Hazel and Jefferson), eighty four-

room apartments next door and fifty duplexes at Fairview
Terrace. He has built hundreds of other houses, forty percent
of them for white people, and he is former president of the
National Builders and Brokers Association.

Except for Atlanta University the Akins might have settled somewhere else. He did take coaching jobs from time to
time at Howard and Fiske Universities. But they stayed in
Atlanta, building a handsome modern home for themselves
in the new housing development where most of their apartment buildings are situated.

Their relationship with the white community has been on a
live-and-let-live basis. Their brief flier in the entertainment
business is an illustration. For a while the Waluhaje Apartments presented Sunday afternoon concerts by such Negro
jazzmen as Louis Armstrong and Dizzy Gillespie in a basement room originally intended for a supermarket. They were
suspended suddenly in the year 1959 and I asked Mr. Akin
why.

"We hope it's only temporary," he said gently. "But since
the school integration question seems so tense and so many
white people came to our programs, we thought it best.
There's no use antagonizing the radical element."

He went on, after a pause, to voice his theory about race
relations.

"The white man lives on one hill and the Negro lives on
the other. We've got to come down in the valley and talk
and pray together as children of God."

Mr. Akin's symbolic hill is an actual one in the case of Atlanta University. Its site was known as Diamond Hill in the
old days because of the diamond-shaped conformation at the
intersection of West Mitchell and Tatnall Streets. The school

attained the hill after a humble beginning in a boxcar, where
some New England missionaries started teaching in 1865. Today it is a graduate school offering M.A. and M.S. degrees and
drawing, along with the other five schools, support from such
philanthropists as the Rockefellers, the Mellons and Atlanta's own Robert W. Woodruff.

Atlanta University and five undergraduate colleges associated with it have given some distinguished citizens to the
world. Mattiwilda Dobbs, daughter of a railroad mail clerk,
who went on to star at the Met, was graduated there. (Ironically, she has not sung with the Met in her hometown, con-
fining herself to church concerts where the audience is not
segregated.) Mordecai Johnson, president of Howard College,
is one of about twenty-five college presidents who received
part of their education on Diamond Hill.

W. E. B. DuBois, the first Negro to receive the degree of
doctor of philosophy from Harvard (1895) began teaching at
Atlanta University in 1896 where, according to Rayford W.
Logan (*The Negro in the United States*) he started "a series
of studies that are indispensable for an understanding of the
Negroes' struggle for equal rights and . . . established beyond reasonable doubt the capacity of a trained Negro to compete on equal terms with other Americans in the realm of
scholarship." He was called "the greatest intellect of his
race" at that time and "one of the great minds of the United
States."

James Weldon Johnson, the poet and first national organ-
izer and executive secretary of the NAACP, was graduated
from Atlanta University in 1894. Walter White, his successor,
was also an Atlanta University graduate, as was Fletcher Henderson, the Cuthbert, Georgia, farm boy whose postgraduate

work in chemistry and math were interrupted in New York when he met W. C. Handy. As students of Jazz know, "Fletch" Henderson played a little piano for Handy, became a jazz bandleader and what many regard as the best jazz arranger of all time. He wrote arrangements for Isham Jones, the Dorsey brothers and Benny Goodman and served as accompanist to Ethel Waters.

The University Center draws many celebrities, white and Negro. Dr. Ralph Bunche lectured there many times, W. S. V. Tubman, President of Liberia, on a state visit to this country, dropped by to see Atlanta, the birthplace of his mother, and stayed on a few days at Atlanta University. Marian Anderson sang her first concert for pay here in 1919. It was a fifty-dollar fee. In 1952 twenty-five multimillionaires, including Richard K. Mellon, John D. Rockefeller, III, Harvey Firestone, Jr., and Winthrop Aldrich—as well as the local Robert W. Woodruff—spent a day touring the campuses of the five Negro colleges. (Their bread-and-butter note a few days later was a contribution of five million dollars.) The Rockefellers have been big and steady contributors to the schools, particularly Spelman College, for many years.

Most members of Atlanta's white community are only dimly aware of these goings and comings. They are more aware of a diplomat—Atlanta University's president, Dr. Rufus Clement.

Dr. Clement is a member of the Atlanta City Board of Education and he got there because thousands of white people along with presumably all the 10,000 registered Negro voters cast a ballot for him in 1953 and in every election since then.

He ran on a platform of experience—thirty-six years as an

educator, twenty-two as president of Atlanta University and the rest as a teacher of history. Although he enjoys positions of honor in the nation and is received as a cultivated gentleman in homes and clubs when he travels abroad or in the north, Dr. Clement conducts himself with a quiet dignity that just misses being diffidence when he appears in public in the South. This is not through any lack of conviction as to the rights of his race but is perhaps a mixture of diplomacy and natural courtesy.

Dr. Clement was born in the South, in Salisbury, North Carolina, attending Livingston College from which both his father, a Methodist bishop, and his mother, the only Negro woman ever named American Mother of the Year, were graduated. (Their graduation was also their wedding day.)

He went to Northwestern University to get his master's and doctor's degrees with the idea of following his father into the ministry. But an after-school job working with boys at a Chicago settlement house showed him that his real vocation lay with young people and may have pointed up a need one of his predecessors at Atlanta University took as a battle cry: "Educate! Educate! Educate!"

At any rate, young Rufus Clement switched from preaching to teaching and has never regretted either that or the fact that his hometown is the capital of the Deep South. For he has been known to turn down United Nations assignments in various parts of the world for a reason incomprehensible to his sympathetic white friends: He loves Atlanta.

Faulty as it is, he loves it. This love is a curiously touching blend of pride and trust. He is proud of the attitude of Atlanta officials, particularly Police Chief Herbert Jenkins and his force who, he says, except for rare and isolated instances, are scrupulously fair in their treatment of Negroes.

He thought Atlanta stores accorded Negro customers the same treatment shown white customers, except in the matter of restaurant and restroom facilities, before they were integrated. In fact, he had rather shop at Muse's, one of the city's older and better men's outfitters, than at New York's famed Brooks Brothers for the cozy reason that he knows and is known to the clerks at Muse's and can be more easily suited.

He insists that he believes in the future of Atlanta because of the "common sense and goodwill" of its leaders. If he has suffered any slights he doesn't mention them.

"You can't do your best work if you're going to be sensitive," he says.

This attitude parallels one of a woman who is probably Atlanta's favorite representative of the Negro community—poised, soft-voiced Grace Towns Hamilton, daughter of one Atlanta University professor, and wife of another. For many years the executive director of the Atlanta Urban League, Mrs. Hamilton is now a consultant on community planning. She has worked patiently and indefatigably for better conditions for Negroes, and each gain, from the matter of treatment facilities for private patients at Grady Hospital to the big cooperative Negro housing development—first of its kind in the nation—has been hard won.

A woman of learning and great personal charm, Mrs. Hamilton has escaped the stigma of the meddlesome, aggressive, unrealistic "do-gooder" by some quality of quiet reason which gets respect, sometimes grudging respect, in the highest places. A businessman not usually sympathetic to Mrs. Hamilton's projects, one day ordered an investigation of an incident of alleged brutal treatment of a Negro at a quiet-spoken suggestion from her.

"I wouldn't believe it happened," he said. "But I'll investigate because Mrs. Hamilton called me. Grace Hamilton doesn't go off half-cocked."

For her part Grace Hamilton is sustained as much by her sense of irony as her patience. I happened by one day when a group of young Negro women who had been working to get better lunchroom and restaurant facilities for Negroes in a big downtown store, asked for advice. They had called upon the head of the store and submitted their request, which he had received courteously and promised to do something about.

What he had done, they wailed to Mrs. Hamilton, had fallen far short of what they had asked. They were terribly disappointed and they didn't know what to say.

"Never mind," Grace comforted them. "You've made a start. Now you must call the man and thank him for the 'improvement.'"

The slowly improving financial situation of Negro citizens and the growth of a solid middle class may accomplish faster what diplomacy, the conference table and suits in Federal Court have been unable to do. All members of the Darker Third are aware of this and they would be unnatural if they didn't enjoy the coup of a well-to-do Negro woman who built a new home and had it decorated—to the tune of many thousands of dollars—by a local store. When the bill came and the customary courtesy title, Mrs., was missing from the envelop, she called the store and sent everything back.

"More Normal than Usual"

CHAPTER VII

On August 29, 1961, the Atlanta Police Department's bulletin, a mimeographed newssheet issued daily to more than seven hundred officers carried this announcement:

"In accordance with Federal and State regulations and under orders from the Federal Courts the Atlanta schools will be desegregated when schools open on August 30, 1961.

"If there are any objections to the manner and method of operation of the Atlanta Public Schools those objections must be made to the superintendent of schools office at City Hall and under no circumstances will objections, discussion or disturbance be permitted at any of the individual schools."

Very matter-of-factly the bulletin noted that "Hate" literature would probably be distributed and that representatives of "Hate" organizations might be on the scene. It listed the names and addresses of these individuals.

Toward the bottom of the page there was another list—the

names and addresses of the Negro students and the schools each planned to attend.

A score card, a cop remarked later, "so we'll know the players."

But that wasn't all. The bulletin reminded the officers of their duty:

"The highest value of the law is the keeping of the peace. The Atlanta Police Department has full responsibility and authority to maintain the peace and good order over the entire city and especially at and around the schools."

The bulletin concluded by citing chapter and verse of that authority from local and state laws. It was signed by Herbert Jenkins, chief of police.

What happened in Atlanta on August 30, 1961, is now known throughout the world. The public schools were integrated peacefully. The next day newspapers all over the nation editorially hailed this Deep South city's "display of sanity and good sense."

The Police Department had planned and performed as their bulletin indicated they would—calmly, watchfully, meticulously "keeping the peace."

That bulletin, of course, was by no means the cause of Atlanta's peaceful school integration. It was, instead, the effect of a community attitude, of cumulative forces a long time abuilding.

There were times in the days leading up to August 30, 1961, when it appeared that Atlanta might have gone either way. To many old-guard southerners, breaking the traditional patterns of segregation was unthinkable. To some the very word "integration" was a dirty word connoting all kinds of hideous social evils, ranging from syphilis to consorting with Communists. Many people believed sincerely that if by any chance the South had not yet provided "separate but equal" schools, housing, health and recreation facilities for the races, it could and would, if let alone.

Two men knew better. One was an idealist, Ralph Emerson McGill, editor of the Atlanta *Constitution* from 1940 to 1960 and now publisher. The other was a practical politician, William Berry Hartsfield, who ended twenty-three years as Mayor of Atlanta the first of January 1962.

McGill, long before the 1954 decision of the Supreme Court, had been attacking the inequities from the side of conscience.

"I wish those among us who are always so ardent in defense of their own interpretation of Southern traditions would be ardent in the defense of the Southern tradition which says that we always treat the Negro fairly," he wrote back in 1947 when the city spent fifty thousand dollars on a saddle ring for white citizens at Chastain Park and there was no park at all for Negroes.

"We don't and we never have given him a square rattle in education, before the bar of justice or in housing or in public parks. We have laws which separate the races but the same laws call for equal accommodations in facilities and transportation and we have cheated on that too. Yet if you begin to discuss such things, the clamor arises about 'social equality' and 'nigger loving' and the fearful run for cover."

Mayor Hartsfield wasn't so vocal about the rights and wrongs of the question but he felt very strongly about what was good for Atlanta. From the time Negroes first began to push for small gains—members on the police force, the right to use city golf courses—when the Mayor acted in their behalf, his political enemies might call him "nigger-loving" and the NAACP candidate, but the Negroes themselves knew better.

"Make no mistake," a Negro leader once said. "Mr. Hartsfield is by no means our Great White Father. He is simply a very practical man."

The Mayor had no apology for that.

"When you stop to hate," he has said again and again, "you stop all constructive work."

The golf course issue came up in 1957 with a U. S. Supreme Court decision. Mayor Hartsfield knew it would be invoked in Atlanta at any time and he got ready. He observed in cities where the golf courses were already integrated that relatively few Negroes played anyhow because it was a leisurely, time-consuming game. So he called a meeting of city parks employees to discuss the ruling and pointed out two simple home truths:

1) If the court order was not complied with the golf courses would close.

2) If they closed, one hundred white employees would lose their jobs and seventy thousand white users of the public links would lose a place to play.

Then in the courts he fought a delaying action aimed at one little known thing—to get the compliance date moved to the Christmas season.

"It's not easy for people to hate each other at Christmas time," he pointed out. "It's the time of year of universal goodwill. I couldn't believe we'd have any unpleasant incident then—and we didn't."

Being both a practical and an imaginative man, Mayor

Hartsfield took another little precaution. He called the Negro leader who had filed the suit and asked him not to begin his golf game at the time and the place announced where cameras and television crews would be assembled. It would avert a possible demonstration, he pointed out. The Negro doctor and his golfing companions agreed and two days before Christmas they teed off on the city-owned Bobby Jones Golf Course without fanfare and without incident.

The desegregation of the city's trolleys went almost as smoothly, although in recognition of state Jim Crow laws the police had to arrest the hymn-singing Negroes who boarded the trolleys, Bibles in hand, and sat down on the front seats. Both sides understood what was going to happen, however, and a police lieutenant tells the story of one Negro would-be rider who got to the scene too late to demonstrate. He came panting into headquarters after the paddy wagon had arrived with the Reverend Williams Holmes Borders and his band of demonstrators and was so embarrassed to be left out the police obligingly locked him up with the others.

After the courts ruled, trolley integration went off without a hitch. But there were plenty of hitches elsewhere. Lunchrooms and restaurants in the department, variety and drug stores, normally the refuge of the downtown worker and shopper, closed right and left before the arrival of sit-in-throngs from the Negro youth movement. These were frequently joined by sympathetic students from the white high schools and colleges, which added even more to the ire of White Citizens Council members and similar white supremacy groups. Students picketed the stores, and on occasion the Ku Klux Klan, in full regalia but sans masks, which are prohibited by state law, picketed the pickets.

Through the intercession of the Mayor and the Chamber of Commerce this phase of the conflict ended with the integration of public eating places in the spring of 1962.

Through it all, however, the schools were at the heart of the conflict—all the schools of Georgia eventually, but the schools of Atlanta almost immediately.

U. S. District Judge Frank Hooper had already ordered the City Board of Education to submit a desegregation plan, and when that came back—a stair-step plan to begin with the twelfth grade—he ordered it to take effect in September 1960. Later he added the eleventh grade to that order. State law stood in the way and the legislature's answer was the appointment of a study commission headed by John Sibley, seventy-one, a prominent Atlanta lawyer-banker.

The commission collected opinions for many weeks, meeting in the cities and small towns of the state—and the majority of that opinion was that it was better to close the schools than to desegregate. Nevertheless, the commission's majority report recommended local option on the question.

Local option, as far as one group of Atlanta mothers were concerned, had to be swung to open schools at all costs. These were the women who were to later gain renown as the founders of HOPE (Help Our Public Education). They were a group of mothers who began by being horrified at having their broods at home on their hands all day long *if* the schools closed and went on from there to contemplate the long-range results of no schools.

Like Mayor Hartsfield, Mrs. Hamilton Lokey and Mrs. William Breeden, founders of HOPE, didn't waste any time hashing over the ideological aspects of segregation versus integration. They didn't even consider raising the question of how parents felt about sending their children to school with Negroes. All they wanted to do was to combine forces with parents who were determined to send their children to school, period.

Up until the organization of HOPE, the only people who were making themselves heard with any volume were the Negroes speaking through their court suits and such arch-segregationist groups as the Ku Klux Klan, the White Citizens Council and the newly organized GUTS (Georgians Unwilling To Surrender) and Separate Schools, Inc.

Now other groups began to be heard from. Ministers issued manifestos. There were three in all, signed by a total of several hundred ministers, white and Negro, of all faiths.

On Christmas Day 1960, in a special Christmas message, the ministers of the city said in part:

"We cannot ignore the differences which exist among us. It is not likely that we shall soon be fully agreed as to the specific steps which should be taken for the solution of our problems. We are convinced, however, that the only pathway to progress lies in the direction of friendship, of respect for the convictions of others and of determination to maintain communications between the leaders of all racial and religious groups within our community."

State leaders maintained their adamant stand against integration, however, until the event which shocked and horrified people in all 159 of the counties of the state: Rioting at the University of Georgia.

Two Negro students, Hamilton Holmes and Charlayne Hunter of Atlanta, presented themselves to the registrar at the university in Athens on January 9 and were admitted as freshmen. Things were apparently going smoothly. They were assigned dormitory rooms and had started their classes and then darkness fell and the mobs gathered.

Local segregationists were joined by imported racists and rabble-rousers. Athens police and sheriff's officers were summoned by the university officials. The State Patrol was called out, rocks sailed through the air, tear gas bombs exploded. Inside the dormitories, girls from all over Georgia cowered in their darkened rooms, uncertain and fearful. The Negro students were sent home for a few days in the interest of peace while state officials pondered what to do.

It was a bitter cold night on Capitol Hill in Atlanta when the legislature convened in "unusual and emergency session" to hear what Governor S. Ernest Vandiver had to say. He had been elected on a firm campaign promise that "no Negro . . . no not one . . . will ever attend a white school in Georgia."

If he adhered to that promise now the university would close, to be followed perhaps in weeks by the closing of schools in Atlanta and then elsewhere in the state.

The Governor's wife and their three school-age children accompanied him down the aisle of the House chamber to the rostrum. They listened attentively to what he had to say.

"These past few days have been trying ones for all of us," he said. "Days of shock, frayed tempers, anger, shouts and even violence, but, over in the distance, through it all shone a steady light—the light of Georgia character, the innate, inbred integrity of our people."

A bit later he continued: "Having seen what can happen in the University System we must move to protect the public schools and Georgia schoolchildren within the legal framework left to us. There is no—NO—sentiment in this state for a blind destruction of public education without offering an effective alternative.

"There never has been.

"Every legal means and resource to circumvent the effects of the decision, yes. Defiance, no. Private schools offered as a last resort, yes. Destruction of education, no. That has been the policy. That is the policy today. Our course is lawful resistance—not defiance—not violence."

Mandatory school-closing statutes were repealed, and a package of open-school bills were passed in their place.

The crisis was by no means over, but Charlayne Hunter and Hamilton Holmes returned to the University of Georgia where they proceeded in peace with their education.

In Atlanta the women in HOPE began promoting public acceptance of the change in tone from the state government. Out of this grew OASIS (Organizations Assisting Schools In September). It embraced fifty-three groups, ranging from civic clubs, labor unions, religious and business and professional organizations to Boy Scouts.

All over town OASIS affiliates held meetings to plan for desegregation. Community discussions were organized. Speakers and literature were provided, community leaders were encouraged to speak out and the campaign reached a climax the weekend before schools opened with "law and order" observances in churches. There were neighborhood coffees and PTA and garden club programs. The Society of Friends (Quakers) even arranged get-togethers for the white and Negro students who would be attending school together "to cushion the transition."

So on August 30, 1961, Atlanta became the first Deep South city to peacefully desegregate its public schools.

The scores of newspaper, magazine and wire service reporters and radio and television representatives who flocked into
town, anticipating another Little Rock or New Orleans, might
have been personally relieved but professionally let down at
the outcome of the story.

Characteristically, Mayor Hartsfield, the old showman,
turned it into an occasion to sell the charms and wonders of
Atlanta to outlanders. Journalists from as far away as London
might have trouble in years to come remembering the details
of ten young Negro boys and girls starting to school with
their white contemporaries in Atlanta. But they probably will
never forget the fantastic handling of that story by the then
mayor.

It was an era, remember, when newspaper photographers
were having their cameras smashed by mobs. Reporters had
their cars overturned, sometimes burned. Members of the
press were often hurt. Later one was to lose his life in Mississippi. And nearly everywhere when all else failed, people
blamed the strife on the presence of the press.

Contrast that to the Hartsfield reception in Atlanta.

The council chamber at City Hall was turned into a gigan-
tic press room with tables, typewriters and telephones for all.
Teletype machines were installed for those who needed them.
A radio system was installed for instant communication with
the principals of each of the five schools and the officers on
duty outside. Mayor Hartsfield, who manned the City Hall
microphone most of the day, spelled from time to time by
School Superintendent John Letson and Assistant Superintendent Rural Stephens, had but to flip a switch and the press
was in communication with the people on the scene—able to
ask questions and hear the answers. There was nothing to be

gained by going out to the schools and constituting a crowd on a sidewalk, although most of us had a try at it. When there was a ripple in the smooth operation and there was a little one—the arrest of four teen-age boys who refused to move on when told to at one of the schools—the people in the council chamber were instantly alerted and taken to police headquarters to see the boys and to hear their stories in court.

Meanwhile in an anteroom to the council chamber the Chamber of Commerce helped the visiting press to stave off starvation by setting forth snacks of Smithfield ham, hot biscuits, coffee and fruit juices and, of course, the ubiquitous Atlanta beverage, Coca-Cola.

Publisher McGill dropped by and Mayor Hartsfield introduced him as the South's "great man" and the architect of Atlanta's peaceable approach to its problems. McGill took a bow, remarking wryly that such fulsome praise was "what you get when you vote for Bill Hartsfield every time."

When school was out and the last piece of copy had been moved, buses provided by the transit company whirled up to take the guests on a tour of the city, with the Mayor himself acting as guide. And they came back to a cocktail party whomped up in their honor by the merchants at the Biltmore Hotel.

H. W. Kelly, principal of Northside High School, inadvertently found words to describe the day so long prepared for. Asked at the radio-telephone press conference how things had gone at his school, Mr. Kelly remarked solemnly that as opening days went, that one was "a bit more normal than usual."

Atlantans, Proper and Improper

CHAPTER VIII

"Atlanta Society is like missionary stew," observed a long-time member of it. "If you're in it, you know it. If you're not, you couldn't care less."

The shattering experience of an Atlanta woman who was in it and knew it offers another summation of Society-with-a-capital-S.

She went to a party at the home of an old friend—a party specifically planned by the hostess to present her new daughter-in-law to the women who would be her mentors and her peers in her new home. This elderly guest was received, welcomed rather warmly, as befitted her status, introduced and was well into the petits fours when she remembered that she had promised to pick up a friend on the way to the party. Not wishing to interrupt her hostess she slipped quietly out the back door, sent her chauffeur to retrieve the other guest and re-entered through the front door. Before she could ex-

plain, she was again warmly received, welcomed and introduced.

"My dear, she didn't even know I had *already arrived!*" this
lady related, more in sorrow than censure. "It just shows you
that Atlanta has grown so fast nobody notices any more where
you've been, where you're going or WHO you are!"

Some old-timers will tell you it was ever thus in Atlanta.
Since before Sherman, of the three—where you've been, where
you're going and who you are—the greatest of these has been
where you're going.

In the early days the fact that you came to Atlanta at all
was a good indication that you were going somewhere. Those
who didn't have energy and drive, spunk and ambition, stayed
where they were—in older, well-established cities of the North
and South. Even after Sherman's departure those who came
were often driven by another success-maker—desperation.
They had nothing behind them except charred lands and
burned-out homes or ruined businesses. They came for the express purpose of making good.

Of course, those who got a head start promptly tried to im-
pose the ancient probationary bans on newcomers. But even
then the time was shorter than it is in most southern cities.

A story told about a member of the famous Nunnally's
candy family illustrates that.

One of the Nunnally wives, herself both beautiful and wellborn, was, according to the tale, showing a visitor about Atlanta and they passed the handsome Druid Hills mansion
built by the founder of a big bakery and the father of a famous
little cake which Atlanta children used to regard as a magnificent delicacy.

The visitor admired the house and inquired about the family until his guide felt obliged to tell him that they were rich but, since the father was a baker, socially inconsequential.

"What is the difference," mused the visitor, "between cakes and candy?"

To which the candy heiress replied with prompt and graceful good humor: "One generation."

A generation by some standards makes an Old Family in Atlanta. But the student of Atlanta Society must not overlook the fact that there are families who were here before 1865 and were bonafide, card-carrying aristocrats when they arrived. They had stature in that pushing, grabbing frontier era and they retained it after the war, when the rebuilding began, for any one of several reasons. They had come from sacked plantations or dead small towns seeking their fortunes, but they had grown up with "advantages" and had education, agreeable manners and some artistic attainments. Or they were the near kin of men who had already attained prominence somewhere else in the professions, in politics or in war.

Frank Daniel, the Atlanta newspaperman who came from a small Georgia town and has been an interested and amused observer of Atlanta Society for more than a quarter of a century, says he once knew a lady who was neither beautiful nor wealthy nor interesting. But she flourished on the Atlanta social scene nevertheless because: "*Both* her grandfathers were Confederate generals! She was absolutely impenetrable!"

This group might have become Atlanta's Society. Indeed, it *was* Atlanta Society for a while, establishing at least one still-prevailing rule for women who would succeed socially: Do good works.

The earliest Atlanta social leaders, unlike those in San

Francisco, New York and New Orleans, weren't the women who gave the most elegant and interesting parties. They might have been practitioners of the art of fashionable entertaining, except that history took a hand. They hardly had time to raise white columns and get their magnolia and tea olive trees in the ground when The War made ostentatious use of these homes not only bad taste but a sacrilege. Homes became hospitals for the Confederate wounded; such entertaining as went on was for the benefit of the brave men in gray. And erstwhile stylish hostesses became patriotically shabby, stripping themselves of their jewelry to be exchanged abroad for drugs and ammunition.

Not only did the town's nice women go threadbare and unadorned in early days, but when the fighting was over they went into the trenches and brought back and buried the unburied dead.

The first organization of the leading matrons of Atlanta was the Ladies Memorial Association, a body dedicated to preserving and decorating the Confederate graves and observing Confederate Memorial Day each April 26.

Naturally these ladies did not remain the town's social leaders—although the Association is still extant and active— any more than that small core of Old South aristocrats retained the helm of Society in general. Death vanquished the initial set, and although some of their descendants are still around and still prominent—bearing now the additional luster of Old Family status—many have fallen into obscurity or, worse yet, moved away, to be supplanted by newcomers perhaps more gifted than they at the twin arts of making money and making friends.

The United Daughters of the Confederacy and the Daughters of the American Revolution, socially important groups in the beginning, now devote themselves to their original function of patriotic endeavor. Since the lifeblood of any capital-S Society is exclusiveness, the fertility of the fighting men of both wars cost these organizations their grip on Atlanta Society.

As one devoted member of both the UDC and DAR admitted plaintively: "How can we be *anybody* any more? There are so many of us! By now there must be millions of Daughters!"

But the pattern set by the earliest leaders in Atlanta—good works for nice women—survives. Atlanta Society has no idle rich. From the time they are young girls working in the Girls Circle for Tallulah Falls School until they make their debut at the Piedmont Driving Club, Atlanta women are caught up in Good Works.

This may take the form of one of the Junior League's many enterprises—the most impeccable, socially speaking, of all Good Works. It could include membership on one or more boards of charitable organizations. (The A. G. Rhodes Home, a terminal hospital for the incurably ill, was founded by and continues to be operated by a board which started out as the Debutante Club of 1911.) It would most certainly include work for the Red Cross, Community Services or the Henrietta Eggleston Children's Hospital, and either active work in or support of the Symphony Guild, the Music Club and the Atlanta Art Association. (The choice—work or support—naturally depends upon whether the lady has the more financial ability or physical stamina.)

Garden clubs, like "the Daughters," are too numerous to constitute éclat in Atlanta, but because the first garden club in America was organized at Athens, Georgia, by the ladies of several distinguished, white-columned families, this organization enjoys rather more social prestige here than in many cities. And until they get so old and tired they seek refuge in apartment life, most Atlanta women feel obliged to belong to a garden club, usually their mother's. This serves the purpose of Good Works, in that the garden clubs keep beautiful many small parks and the grounds of charitable institutions and sponsor several flower shows a year. It also gives the beginning homemaker the confidence to cope with some irascible, dark-skinned old yardman by whose side, if she is lucky, she will trudge through the autumns and springs of her middle years, spreading sheep manure, mulching camellias, and trampling out a vintage of glorious greensward and flowering borders.

Their devotion to Good Works has by no means made leaders of Atlanta Society a bunch of lackluster bluestockings. As one delightful old lady, now in her seventies, explained after an evening of dancing the samba at the Capitol City Club: "Atlanta people love a romp. Always have. Surely you've heard of Lucy Peel?"

Lucy Peel, more frequently and deferentially referred to as Mrs. William Lawson Peel, died in 1923, but her name is still a legend in Atlanta. She was a ruling queen in Atlanta Society at the turn of the century and the author of a variety of civic causes, some of which were so impressive the Chamber of Commerce once gave a banquet in her honor.

The only memorable thing surviving about that affair today is a story which Margaret Mitchell circulated joyfully in her youth. The official charged with paying oratorical tribute to Mrs. Peel became so drunk on his own eloquence or so captivated by the honor guest's charm that he finished off his address in this wise: "And in the future, Mrs. Peel, no matter what you do, remember, *the chamber is behind you!*"

Margaret Mitchell was, during her teen-age and debutante years, a pet of the older woman's, frequently regally singled out to serve in a sort of acolyte capacity in some of Mrs. Peel's Good Works.

They apparently had a great deal in common, Mrs. Peel and Peggy Mitchell, being bold and ardent spirits both. But the association suffered a severe setback when Peggy was commanded to get together some of her young friends and put on a program to entertain Mrs. Peel's adored Joseph Habersham Chapter of the DAR. Either wearying of the demands made on her or motivated by mischief, Peggy enlisted the aid of one of her more Bohemian cronies, dressed herself up like a Parisian strumpet and staged for the horrified Daughters a torrid apache dance.

It was precisely the kind of thing Mrs. Peel herself might have done in her younger days, but perversely—and probably because it offended her precious DAR chapter, which she truly loved—Mrs. Peel was monumentally outraged and summarily banished her young aide.

Ironically, Mrs. Peel herself is credited with having engineered a similar caper which produced pandemonium in Atlanta musical circles, put at least a momentary crimp in the career of Met Diva Geraldine Farrar and resulted in ministers mounting the pulpit to denounce the decline of morals among the upper classes.

Mrs. Peel and her husband, gentle, dignified Colonel William Lawson Peel, who was president of the American National Bank, were among the early sponsors of the Metropolitan Opera in Atlanta. Out of a music festival staged in 1909 and starring Geraldine Farrar, a movement started to bring the Met to town. Miss Farrar herself gave impetus to the movement by confiding to a local gentleman who came to take her automobile-riding that an opera singer feels "stiff and constrained" performing without the costumes, scenery and acting opportunities of a Met production.

"Why don't you people have the opera—the Metropolitan Company?" asked Miss Farrar. And Atlantans, led by Colonel Peel, who was subsequently renowned as "the father of grand opera in Atlanta," spun into action, headily wooing the Met into coming to Atlanta, replete with Enrico Caruso and a return engagement by Miss Farrar.

It was the beginning of a long-time love affair for Atlanta and opera—one which continues to this good day with the Met's spring appearance constituting the perennial high point in each year's social season. But it hit a dilly of a snag in April 1920, thanks largely to Mrs. Peel.

Madame Farrar, essaying the role of Zaza in the opera of that name, had a mind to bring considerable verve and audacity to the role of the hoydenish sex queen. She thought the seductress might do a partial strip on stage and she sought counsel of Mrs. Peel to determine how far she might safely go with a Bible Belt audience.

"Go the limit," Mrs. Peel rashly advised her.

What Geraldine Farrar did that April day in 1920 might not horrify audiences conditioned to Jayne Mansfield and Marilyn Monroe, but it rocked Mrs. Peel's set. The singer not only took off a great many clothes essential to modesty, she flirted up her skirts and sprayed her teddies with perfume!

It was a great day for the men in the audience who had been dragged unwillingly to the performance. Never, reported the *Journal's* O. B. Keeler, had Atlanta men dreamed that Culture could be so exciting. But Atlanta women and Atlanta preachers were first stunned and then vociferous in their condemnation. Miss Farrar, reprimanded by the Met, blamed the Peels. A preacher, quoted in the New York *Times,* called it an arrant effort to inflame baser emotions and foretold for Atlanta a place in history next to Sodom and Gomorrah.

Geraldine Farrar never came back to Atlanta with the Met. Some years later she scheduled a concert appearance here, but it had to be canceled because the church auditorium where the series was held was forbidden to her.

Mrs. Peel, for once, was very quiet. She may have thought the whole furor senseless, she may have enjoyed it, and then again she may have been thinking about something else.

For although she was unique in many respects, Mrs. Peel was representative of Atlanta women leaders in her passionate espousal of civic projects. In a day when the Victorian notion that nice women didn't let their names be used in the newspapers was still prevalent, Mrs. Peel wrote several hundred signed newspaper articles taking the city fathers to task for the condition of the streets, urging increased recognition and use of Georgia products and campaigning for the betterment of highways and the construction of a Department of Archives to preserve the state's historical records.

Her literary talents were recognized by no lesser personage than the famed editor Henry W. Grady, who lived next door to the Peels. Grady frequently wrote his newspaper stories, editorials and speeches at home and then walked by and asked Mrs. Peel to read and criticize them. She was interested in history in general but particularly in family history and wrote three volumes of genealogy. She headed a society to raise

funds for fatherless children of France during World War I
and was state chairman of a National League of Woman's
Service for the war effort.

Mrs. Peel was no beauty, but she was an arresting dark-eyed
woman who wore magnificent dresses and hats and rouged
her superb bosom to show it off to rosy advantage in the chiffon blouses of the day. Her parties in the Victorian house at
the corner of Peachtree Street and Forrest Avenue were tri-
umphs either of elegance or of informal high jinks in which
she draped herself in an old curtain and romped through amateur theatricals with her children. The town's first kindergar-
ten was organized at her house and the first theatrical group,
the Players Club, met there.

Miss Isma Dooly, the *Constitution*'s society editor, ex-
tended herself to describe Mrs. Peel's clothes and Mrs. Peel's
parties. She wrote of one reception which "almost surpassed
the usual hospitality of this gracious home which is noted for
the elegance of its entertainment." She described the food
as "not only sweets and similar dainties but large platters of
substantial delicacies like salads, pressed meats, the accompanying jellies, richly dressed cold dishes and several hot
courses, all with wines."

"Mrs. Peel," she added, "who makes the wittiest of hostesses was elegantly gowned in white satin, the coat effect
showing a blouse of chiffon and thread lace."

But the time Mrs. Peel's gown attracted the most attention, *without* making the press, was the time she went to a
large party in her shroud.

The Peels had a white housekeeper named Jane Gregory,
who came from the mountains. With the old mountaineer's
distrust of Negro servants, Jane insisted on keeping all the

family silver and food under lock and key. On the day of a party which she wished to attend, Mrs. Peel discovered that Jane had also locked up all her clothes. She had not only locked up the closets and wardrobes and hidden the key but she further complicated matters by suffering a mild stroke and taking to her bed.

The Peels' daughter, Marion, wife of Dr. Phinizy Calhoun, was giving a reception for members of Chi Phi fraternity, which was having a national meeting in Atlanta.

"Mama said she couldn't come," Mrs. Calhoun related. "She couldn't make Jane tell her where the keys were and she couldn't get at her clothes."

The party was in full swing, however, when Mrs. Calhoun looked out across the assembled guests and saw her mother sweeping regally in—a vision in a pink brocade dress she'd had stitched up to be buried in!

Her family recognized it as the shroud she kept in a box in the attic and Mrs. Peel made no effort to deceive the other guests, some of whom still speak in tones of awe of the fascinating woman who waltzed the evening away in gala grave clothes.

When she died at the age of seventy-two, Mrs. Peel was, as she had planned, buried in the pink brocade with its blue bows.

Mrs. Peel has her detractors—men and women now grandparents who still smart at some snub or social defeat she dealt them in their youth. She was too outspoken and too contentious to be universally beloved. Her children and grandchildren found life with her strenuous, exacting and spellbinding. They couldn't bear to leave home or even to be sick because of the terrible risk of missing something. A sofa in the

parlor was designated the "Disease Couch" because unless
they were delirious or highly infectious, it was where every
member of the family, including Mrs. Peel herself, chose to
remain while ill.

Mrs. Peel had her organized charities and what her family
calls her disorganized charities. She always kept an artist in
the basement. They were practically always hungry and only
occasionally talented, but in order to keep them busy Mrs.
Peel made the children and unresisting friends sit for their
portraits.

She responded warmheartedly when she heard of trouble,
although her generosity did not always take the most practical
form. Once some distant cousins of hers lost everything they
owned in a fire which burned down their home. Mrs. Peel
sent them word to hang on and be of stout heart, she had
help on the way. Very soon a great big box did arrive from
Lucy Peel. The cousins hurriedly opened it to find she had
sent them one dozen gorgeous plumed and flower-decked
picture hats.

Mrs. Peel is but one Atlanta woman, more spirited than
some, more dominant than many, but in a way representative
of the Atlanta-style of southern society leader. A daughter of
rural aristocracy whose father was the Confederate General
Philip Cook, she had what was in her era, and still is, the
approved background for this leadership. She came from the
country, Schley County, by way of Wesleyan College and
sojourns with well-placed cousins in an older city, Macon.
She exhibited early what Atlanta has always liked—a nice
blend of reverence for the past and hearty delight in the
present. Gaiety and sociability pleased but by no means absorbed her. Her gifts were engaged in an arena larger and

more important than the drawing room: the City of Atlanta, the State of Georgia, the economic, civic and cultural betterment of the region.

There were leaders before Mrs. Peel and there have been some since her, but the pattern remains little changed.

Miss Isma Dooly is perhaps the closest thing Atlanta ever had to a society editor–social arbiter. Miss Isma, assisted by her sister, Louise, and later by the delightful Bessie Shaw Stafford, ran the women's department of the *Constitution* from 1895 to her death in 1921. In a fluid, changing society she was a fixed figurehead, and some of her readers came to depend upon her to decide who was and who was not Atlanta Society. For favored newcomers like William Randolph Hearst, who bought the Atlanta *Georgian* in 1912 and published it for twenty-seven years, eventually selling out to owners of the *Journal*, Miss Dooly sometimes determined the tone of a party by dictating the guest list.

But her interest went far beyond balls and euchre parties. She championed the organization of women's clubs as a means of tackling public measures. She developed what was new in the South—a sound woman's page of general interest, backing every measure involving welfare and advancement of women and children. She was especially interested in Negro children and poor mountain children and she labored to get women admitted to the University of Georgia. A plaque on the first women's dormitory on the university campus and an auditorium bearing her name at the Tallulah Falls School for mountain children are testimony to the intelligence, energy and humanity of a magnetic woman who thought social betterment more important than Society.

Although she was no beauty and no belle, Miss Dooly attracted men readers and had many men friends, who enjoyed her conversation and were swayed by her convictions. Atlanta was very gay during the years when Miss Isma covered society, maybe gayer than it has been since. Telamon Cuyler, celebrated turn-of-the-century *bon vivant*, once tabulated the parties he went to during a seven weeks winter period.

Just to contemplate his list is enough to make any present-day sit-by-the-television socialite limp with fatigue.

"I went to the following affairs, large and small," wrote Mr. Cuyler, and he listed: "Four cotillions, one bal masque, sixteen dances, one hop, one soirée, one question party, one musicale, nine evening theater parties, one matinée party, nineteen dinners, thirteen receptions, twenty-six teas, two stag dinners, four buffet luncheons, three Christmas parties, four eggnog parties, two children's parties, one surprise birthday party, two charity pay affairs, eight club affairs, four winter wheel [bicycle] meets, one New Year's party, one breakfast and eleven suppers."

Members of Atlanta's Old Guard, in the fashion of Old Guard everywhere, look on those days as the halcyon days of Society. Sometimes over their whiskey sours at the Piedmont Driving Club they speak mournfully to Julius Gaines—the aging Negro factotum who has been at the club longer than most of the members—of another time and another city. Sometimes, like one elderly, erstwhile belle, they play out renunciation scenes.

"Atlanta's not my town any more," this lady says, savoring nostalgia along with her bourbon. "The tackpots have taken over."

Tackpot may not be a term in the vocabulary of the New

York, Newport or Boston hostess, but it is expressive enough for Atlantans. Taken from the root word "tacky," meaning gauche and tasteless, tackpot designates the Johnny-Come-Lately, the district manager, the regional representative—the whole new segment of population that moved in from Illinois and Iowa and Salt Lake City to cause new subdivisions and schools and shopping centers to pop out like lightning bugs on a summer night; to join the old clubs or organize new ones, to give parties and go to them.

Far from being literal tackpots, some of these people are fully as charming and knowledgeable as the Old Guard—frequently more so. Their only impediment is one they themselves can't see—they don't remember-when.

"*Peggy's Book*"

CHAPTER IX

If Atlantans were to speak of The Good Book they would, in all probability, mean the Bible. When they speak of The Book, there's no question. They mean *Gone With the Wind.* A cozy, more local name still in fairly common usage is "Peggy's book."

The querulous suggestion, sometimes voiced, that we make a good deal out of *Gone With the Wind* in this neck of the woods is no more true than the suggestion, for instance, that Carl Sandburg got hold of a molehill and turned it into a mountain of Lincolniana.

For the evidence is indisputable that *Gone With the Wind* was and is a phenomenon. It has been translated into twenty-seven languages, including the Arabic, copped most major literary prizes, including the Pulitzer, sold more than ten million copies, and was made into a movie which even now, nearly twenty-five years after its release, is always playing somewhere in the world.

Margaret Baugh, the author's secretary, who still keeps nine-to-five hours in a downtown office handling correspondence with publishers in the far corners of the world and details of litigation against publishers in Iron Curtain countries who keep pirating it, once said of the movie: "It's like the former British Empire. The sun never seems to set on it."

A man in Denmark has two excursion boats named for Scarlett and Melanie, the heroines of the book. A publisher from the Netherlands came to Atlanta a few years ago expressly to put a basket of flowers on the grave of the author. Huntington Hartford, III, the Great Atlantic and Pacific Tea Company heir, telephoned from California one day a few years back to beg a sample of Peggy's handwriting to study for clues to her character. Hardly a week passes that the Chamber of Commerce is not asked for directions to Tara, Aunt Pittypat's house and Belle Watling's establishment or if Margaret Mitchell's home is open to the public.

All these tangible evidences that *Gone With the Wind* was a very special book are a source of pride to Atlantans. But even dearer to the home folks is recurring evidence that Peggy's book established a peculiar rapport between Georgians and people in all parts of the world. Wherever people have suffered war and subjugation Margaret Mitchell's story of survival in the South has intensely personal meaning. It dramatized for citizens of sacked cities the world over that Atlanta was also a city—the only American city—totally destroyed by war and rebuilt.

Actually, for those earnest, admiring pilgrims who come to pay tribute to Margaret Mitchell and the *GWTW* char-

acters, there's practically no physical shrine left in Atlanta.
By Miss Mitchell's express instructions her girlhood
home was torn down. There is no Tara, and never was one,
except the movie set. A boardinghouse named for Aunt Pittypat on Peachtree at Fourth was recently torn down. The
closest thing to Belle Watling's place is probably her modern
counterpart in the oldest profession, the hotel with girls "on
call."

There's a grammar school named for Margaret Mitchell
and a new street. Smith College Alumnae Club annually
gives a scholarship in her name to some deserving Georgia
girl. (The author herself attended Smith only a year and then
came home to look after her father. But after *GWTW* she
was invited back and awarded an honorary degree.) The Atlanta Public Library has a small room dedicated to her memory with an illuminated photograph of the author presiding
over some glass cases containing a first edition and some
foreign editions of the book, the little portable typewriter on
which it was written, a sample of the manuscript and some
still photographs from the film.

On request the visitor may get from an attendant in the
adjacent Fine Arts Department a small booklet, brought out
by the library in 1954, which contains a short biography of
the author, an account of the book's publication and a story
about the making of the movie. (These were written by
William S. Howland, a former Southern Editor of *Time* and
Life magazines and a long-time friend of Peggy's; Norman S.
Berg, southeastern representative of The Macmillan Company, publishers, and Susan Myrick, an associate editor of the
Macon *Telegraph*, who served as technical adviser on southern accent, manners and customs for the movie production.)

Little else remains except her grave in the family lot in Oakland Cemetery, the battered little desk at which she worked for four years in the Sunday Magazine department of the Atlanta *Journal*, and a ludicrous assortment of relics snatched up avidly by fans at the time her girlhood home was torn down in 1952. These and an office in the Peachtree Arcade Building where her brother, attorney Stephens Mitchell, and Miss Baugh still carry on the vast amount of correspondence, royalty and legal business generated by the book.

This is very nearly as Margaret Mitchell would have wanted it. She probably would have been wildly amused at the way old clawfoot bathtubs, water closets, windows, mantels and paving stones sold when wreckers pulled down the 1912 vintage house at 1401 Peachtree Street to make way for an insurance building. But the demolition of the house was exactly what she wanted.

She abhorred the idea of so-called author's shrines—musty old houses visited by people who never read their books. And she couldn't bear to think of her old home becoming a boardinghouse or having a hot-dog stand in the yard. So she elicited from her husband, John Marsh, and her brother, Stephens, a promise that the survivor would see that the house was pulled down.

Her passionate distaste for having her private papers rummaged through by curious strangers or, worse yet, future biographers, led her husband to burn everything else she ever wrote and all but enough of the *Gone With the Wind* manuscript, notes and chronologies to prove her authorship of the book if it is at any time challenged. These are preserved in a very elaborate arrangement outlined by John Marsh in a codicil to his will, which was filed for probate shortly after his death, May 4, 1952. The papers were sealed in an envelop and locked in a vault at the Citizens and Southern Bank with a trust fund established to pay the rent on the vault and establish and authenticate Peggy's authorship of the big book if the need ever arises.

A curious provision of the will is that if Peggy's authorship is ever challenged and the envelop opened, its contents may go to the Atlanta Historical Society, if it is in existence, or the Public Library. If the papers are never needed to prove that his wife wrote the book and the trust is ended by court or governmental authority, "the papers therein shall be destroyed unopened" and the trust fund shall go to the Atlanta Historical Society.

Such a legal to-do over her work hardly seems in keeping with the picture most of her friends have of the light-hearted, out-going Peggy. They attribute this legalistic policing of her privacy largely to her lawyer brother and her husband, an ex-newspaperman who became advertising director of the Georgia Power Company. But both brother and husband insisted that Peggy did not want her biography written or her unpublished works read.

Mr. Mitchell says she "probably wrote one or two novels besides *Gone With the Wind.*

"They were stashed away because for one reason or another she didn't want to offer them for publication. That's just a guess and I can't say whether they were written before or after *Gone With the Wind.*"

As a matter of fact, Peggy did not want to offer *Gone With the Wind* for publication. She wrote it between 1926 and 1929, let it lie untouched for six years, and even denied that she had a book when Harold S. Latham, Macmillan trade

editor and vice-president, came to Atlanta looking for manu-
scripts in 1935. Medora Field Perkerson, an author who had
been a colleague on the Sunday Magazine before she married
their boss, Angus Perkerson, introduced Mr. Latham to
Peggy with a cautious suggestion that he might ask about her
manuscript. He did and she very "pleasantly but with firm-
ness" got him off the subject, Mr. Latham related.

When she mentioned Mr. Latham's inquiry to her husband later in the day he pointed out that she had nothing
to lose by letting such a pro as a publisher have a look at
her work. A few hours later, just before Mr. Latham was to
depart for San Francisco, he received a call in his hotel room
from Peggy. The sight she made, waiting for him in the
lobby, must have been wonderful. She sat there, a little
woman, overshadowed by a mountainous heap of smudgy,
dog-eared typescript. Mr. Latham rushed out and bought a
suitcase to pack the manuscript in and boarded the train.

Gone With the Wind was on its way.

The book came out June 30, 1936. The casting of the movie
kept the nation in a state of argumentative suspense for a
couple of years and on December 13, 1939—one of Atlanta's
more memorable dates—the world première was held at
Loew's Grand Theater. Slightly more than two thousand
people got in the theater that night, but thousands jammed
the streets to pay tribute to the little author, to Vivien Leigh
and Clark Gable, the cinema Scarlett and Rhett, and half a
dozen other Hollywood luminaries who came to town for the
event.

Amazing fame and fortune had arrived for Margaret
Mitchell and Atlanta basked in it. To Peggy herself it made
little appreciable difference. She and John continued to live

in the second-floor apartment at 1268 Piedmont Avenue, where Margaret Baugh was already installed to help handle correspondence. Peggy, as a friend noted, seemed to buy nothing for herself except a fur coat and a secondhand automobile. But her gifts to others, given quietly, were generous and far-reaching. She dispatched hundreds of food packages to Europe during the war. As her devoted maid, Bessie Jordon, wrote of her after her death:

She Fed the Hungry.
She gave drink to the Thirsty.
She clothed the Naked.
Shelted the out of doors.
Ministered to the Sick and in Prison.

Personal charity, a concern for the ill and needy, had been a habit of life with Margaret Mitchell, even before the book brought her affluence. And although she was reared in comfort, the only daughter of a prominent lawyer, she had known lean days. She and John were married on the Fourth of July 1925, not quite a year after her unhappy, short-lived marriage (1922 to 1925) to Berrien K. Upshaw ended in divorce. John was in heavy debt as the result of a long illness and their combined salaries weren't impressive, but Peggy told her family and friends, "John and I are going to live poor as hell and get out of this jam."

Their first home was what Bill Howland called "a physically dark but intellectually bright" small apartment at 979 Crescent Avenue, just back of the Tenth Street shopping center, which they accurately referred to as "The Dump." It was here that she started writing on her book.

It was four blocks from "The Dump"—on Peachtree Street

at Thirteenth—that she was to be fatally injured the night of August 11, 1949. An automobile driven by an off-duty taxi driver struck Peggy as she and John started across Peachtree Street to see a movie at the Peachtree Art Theater. She died in Grady Hospital five days later. She suffered massive head injuries and never regained consciousness. The taxi driver, Hugh D. Gravitt, twenty-nine at the time, was convicted of involuntary manslaughter and sentenced to from twelve to eighteen months' imprisonment.

Two things helped to convict Gravitt of an accident which may not have been entirely his fault. After all, Peggy had apparently panicked while crossing the street and run into Gravitt's path because John, who stood still and waited, was not grazed by the car. But because Gravitt was photographed smiling when he was docketed at the jail and because he had a record of twenty-five violations, a public outcry which reached around the world sounded against him. The smile was wrongly interpreted to reflect the callous, unrepentant attitude of a killer.

Later, when he was serving time in the Bellwood Public Works camp, I talked to him and found him a desperately unhappy man who had been the victim of his own reflexes.

"A photographer said, 'Smile,'" he told me, "and I did it without thinking. I didn't feel like smiling. If I could I would have been the one in front of that car instead of the one driving it."

As for the traffic violations, they were no more than hundreds of taxi drivers pile up within a few years, hacking in downtown traffic.

As a matter of fact, Gravitt had been on his way to pick up medicine for his sick child when his car struck Georgia's most famous citizen—the beloved "little lady of the big book."

In the end, he served but four months, the requisite time on good behavior, before he was released on parole. But I have an idea that his life was permanently and irreparably scarred.

The deathwatch at Grady Hospital, the leaden hours of waiting in the hall for doctors' bulletins, was a sad experience for those of us who covered it. The funeral (admission by card for three hundred people, most of them old newspaper friends) was very moving. Peggy had been reared a Roman Catholic, but after her divorce and remarriage she departed the church of her childhood. An old friend, the Very Reverend Raimundo de Ovies, retired dean of St. Philip's Cathedral, read the simple Episcopal service in Patterson's Chapel, asking mercy and peace for "thy daughter, Margaret."

Bareheaded multitudes lined the streets to the Mitchell family lot in old Oakland Cemetery, burial ground of founding citizens, but only a handful of flowers graced her coffin. These were roses grown within the walls of Atlanta Penitentiary by her old friends, the prisoners, to whom she had written, spoken and given prizes for literary efforts. At the family's request all others who might have sent flowers sent instead contributions for the treatment of the indigent at Grady Hospital.

It was a time of statewide mourning in Georgia. By order of Governor Herman Talmadge the flag over the capitol flew at half-staff. But from my relatively short acquaintance with the blithe and bumptious little author I think she may have been pleased that I didn't emerge from covering her injury and death without one bright patch of humor to remember.

It was a day or so after the funeral that Frank Daniel, the *Journal* reporter and a long-time friend of the Marshes, and I happened to meet at their apartment in quest of follow-up stories for our respective Sunday papers. (This was before the merger.)

John received us graciously and talked freely. But he was a very deliberate man, given to slow speech and rambling reminiscence. Each of us had questions to ask and were urgently conscious of our deadlines bearing down on us. John seemed to me to take an agonizingly long time with many interminable digressions, and when we finally got the information we came for, Frank and I bolted for the door together.

Outside, mindful of the fact that he was a much older and closer friend of our bereaved host, I daringly remarked that John Marsh was a very long-winded man.

"Yes," said Frank cheerfully. "I always said that Peggy's book, long as it was, was just a snappy comeback to something John had said."

From Whistle to White Mice

CHAPTER X

Sometimes Atlanta doctors, meeting in their handsome Academy of Medicine on West Peachtree Street, make a small bow in the direction of the portrait of a dark-eyed gentleman with whimsical eyes and a high starched collar.

Dr. Joshua Gilbert was their professional ancestor, Atlanta's first doctor—a man whose principal equipment in ministering to a town of five hundred people consisted of a horse, a whistle, a supply of quinine and his own indomitable determination to cure the sick.

Dr. Gilbert came here from South Carolina in 1845, when the town was still called Marthasville, and he stayed until his death in 1889. For a time he was the only doctor and so busy he blew a whistle on his rounds to let people know he was coming. The sound of that little whistle, shrilling night and day, alerted those who might need a doctor and they rushed out to stop him.

Sometimes in his haste he heard their complaints and prescribed without even getting off his horse—literally a horse-back diagnosis. He rolled his own pills, kept no books, collected no accounts and pushed himself so hard his descendants tell of a particularly bitter winter when he almost froze to his saddle and a Negro servant had to pry him loose.

Dr. Gilbert was the forerunner of thousands of doctors, nurses, technicians and researchers who were to make Atlanta a leading, and in some instances unique, medical center in the nation.

That little whistle which must have comforted people in frontier days, reminding even the well that help was near if they needed it, has been succeeded by a complex of more than thirty general and special hospitals, thirteen hundred doctors, one of the country's top medical schools and the U. S. Public Health Service's amazing, one-of-a-kind Communicable Disease Center.

People from all over the Southeast come to Atlanta for treatment. (Hospital administrators say one out of every five patients is from outside the city.) People from all over the world come to confer with researchers at the Communicable Disease Center or to work or teach for a time at Emory University Medical School.

It was from Atlanta that word went out a few years ago that the American Medical Association had determined that smoking was a "causative factor" in cancer. Almost daily our science writers write for local use or dispatch to some professional journal, stories of some new step in the conquest of disease or some suspenseful, even exotic, research project:

A doctor at the Communicable Disease Center has discovered that the right rear footpads of white mice provide growing space for history's first cultivation of human leprosy germs outside the human body. . . . CDC and Emory doctors are working on measles vaccine. . . . Men, mice and chickens are taking doses of insecticides in a long-range study of their hazards. . . . Seventy-nine volunteers check in at Emory for ten days of starvation as part of a study about the process and effects of fasting. . . . A pair of Yugoslavian professors attached to Emory's physiology department are studying hibernation in ground squirrels for the possible effect on human beings fleeing atomic warfare. . . . An assistant professor is looking for the relationship between alcoholism and cirrhosis of the liver. . . . One of the world's leading authorities on primates brings his collection of monkeys to Emory for use in research and teaching, making the University's Yerkes Laboratories in Orange Park, Florida, the first major center for primate research in this country. . . . Seventeen scientists get grants totaling $418,000 for their work in cancer-related fields.

Dramatic and exciting as this era of medicine and research is, Dr. Gilbert could almost have foreseen it for his town. After all, he was a contemporary of the renowned Dr. Crawford W. Long, who pioneered in the use of anesthesia for surgery. Dr. Long's feat was performed in Jefferson, Georgia, in 1842, but he later moved to Atlanta to practice, building a home here in 1851, and today one of the bigger hospitals bears his name. (Jefferson has a museum named for him, containing relics from his practice and a diorama depicting the use of ether in his operations there.)

So swiftly did things move in Atlanta in Dr. Gilbert's day

that nine years after he arrived on horseback, the community's
first doctor, he saw the founding of a medical school. The
Atlanta Medical College, from which Emory University
School of Medicine is descended, was chartered in 1854 and
was ambitiously determined to relieve southern boys of the
necessity of going north to get their medical education.
Things were going along well for the new medical school,
but the Civil War intervened and students and faculty made
haste to join the Confederate forces. (The depth of their feeling is illustrated in a story related by Miss Mildred Jordan,
director of Emory's Abner Wellborn Calhoun Medical
Library. On December 20, 1860, South Carolina seceded
from the Union, and that night Mrs. Willis Westmoreland,
wife of one of the founding doctors at Atlanta Medical
College, gave birth to a daughter. They named the baby
"South Carolina.")

Fans of the book and movie *Gone With the Wind* remember the scenes of terrible suffering when the wounded and dying poured into Atlanta as the fighting got closer. These
scenes are well documented in history. Miss Jordan, writing
in the *Emory Alumnus* in 1961, told how trainloads of the
wounded came in, hospitals and public buildings overflowed
and all families who could were called upon to "accommodate
a wounded soldier" in their homes. The mayor issued a proc-
lamation calling on the businessmen to close their stores at
4 PM so they could meet the trains and help with the
wounded. All Atlanta citizens were "earnestly requested to
send their carriages and their servants to assist in removing
the wounded . . . by night as well as by day."

That was in the summer of 1863 when the fighting was
still some distance from the city. By the spring of '64 when

Sherman began his Atlanta campaign the city was already filled to overflowing with the wounded. And still they came.

Historian Wallace P. Reed's eyewitness account of the city the opening day of the Battle of Atlanta, July 22, is enough to make Miss Mitchell's gutsy fictional version pale. He wrote of seeing General Hood seated on his horse in a little park in front of the Kimball House and near the railroad station, receiving messages "every minute from the scene of action."

Groups of citizens, Reed explains, were gathered in the park watching the general.

"Suddenly the park was invaded by the hospital corps. Long tables were stretched out and a crowd of professional-looking men in uniform took charge of them and commenced opening their cases of instruments. They were surgeons. It was not long before ambulances and wagons rolled into the park by the dozen, and the wounded were hastily taken out and placed upon the tables. After that it was cut and slash, for the work had to be done in a hurry. The green grass took on a blood-red hue, and as the surgeon's saw crunched through the bones of the unfortunates, hundreds of gory arms and legs were thrown into the baskets prepared to receive them."

That night Mrs. Willis Westmoreland gave birth to a son. They called him "Hood."

As Sherman got closer the wounded and dying were evacuated, and by October 7, Federal troops began their ordered destruction of the city. Wounded Federal soldiers had been brought back from the battle of Jonesboro and some of them were placed in the Atlanta Medical College. Dr. Noel

D'Alvigny, a member of the faculty regarded as too old to go to war when the conflict began, found the war had come to him. He worked tirelessly caring for the wounded on both sides—service which later won for him, a French-born "Rebel," commendation from the Federal Government. Although the Federal wounded had been moved out of the Medical College by the military authorities, their presence there must have given the old doctor an idea for saving the school.

According to Historian Reed, Dr. D'Alvigny called in the hospital attendants, plied them with whiskey and put them to bed with instructions to howl in pain when the military arrived. The torch squad came, but Dr. D'Alvigny stood them off.

He had been in three armies, he said, but this was the first time he ever witnessed invaders so depraved as to burn a hospital filled with the wounded. The baffled Yankee officers, who thought everybody had been removed, gave Dr. D'Alvigny until daybreak to get his "patients" out.

But the next morning Sherman's army had started south "and thus, by a ruse, was the valuable building of the Atlanta Medical College saved, to be used again for the noble purpose for which it was first erected."

So the medical profession had a head start on rebuilding when the following April the war ended and people could once more consider peaceful pursuits. The Medical College had been looted of many expensive fixtures and valuable books. Dean Westmoreland's carefully tended "Garden of Medicinal Plants" was a shambles and, Miss Jordan reports, his portrait had evidently been pierced by Minié balls. It hangs today in her custody in the Medical Library, and the holes in the canvas, she has observed, "were patched in such a manner that the dean seems to have a black eye."

The Atlanta Medical College not only flourished but inspired competition. Money was hard come by during Reconstruction days and there were occasions when students, unable to pay their tuition, turned their horses over to the school to be sold. But three other medical schools were to open—Oglethorpe University's in 1870, Southern Medical College in 1887, and the Atlanta School of Medicine in 1903. One at a time they merged with each other and in 1915 became a part of growing Emory University, the little Methodist college which, heavily endowed by Coca-Cola money, today sprawls over beautiful wooded acres in Druid Hills.

The doctors running that early medical school yearned for a hospital and real patients to work on, but they were a long time coming. At one point the medical college operated at its own expense a clinic with hospital facilities and made a deal with the city to treat poor patients, either at the clinic or in their own homes, at a flat rate of fifty cents a day.

Emory's medical students today have no such problems. Its doctors work not only in the handsome Emory University Hospital, located on the campus, but in Henrietta Eggleston Children's Hospital and Aidmore Hospital for Crippled Children, which are connected to Emory by underground tunnels. Crawford W. Long is a community hospital in downtown Atlanta, but Emory owns it and its doctors train there. The Veterans Administration Hospital on Peachtree Road is associated with Emory and is preparing to build a new $15 million facility on Clairmont Road near Emory. Also near Emory Hospital are two former residences which have been converted to a psychiatric clinic for children, where specialists in

that field train. Construction will begin during 1963 on the
$12.5 million State of Georgia Mental Health Center to be
staffed by Emory and built on Briarcliff Road a mile from the
campus.

But the oldest and biggest clinical teaching facility of the
medical school is, of course, old Grady Hospital.

Started in 1892 in a red brick Victorian pile which looks
like a residence out of the gaslight era, old Grady Hospital
is in a way the heart of the city. It was named for Henry W.
Grady, the editor-hero for whom so many things in Atlanta
are named, but it is familiarly called "the Grady's" by indigent Atlantans to whom it has given life. A charity hospital,
operated by the Fulton-De Kalb Hospital Authority and fi-
nanced by taxes, Grady is where everybody, rich or poor, goes
after a brush with violence—crashes, fires, poisonings, shoot-
ings or any other emergency or accidental injury.

Margaret Mitchell's husband, John Marsh, wouldn't permit
an earlier arriving ambulance crew to move her the night she
was struck down by a taxicab on Peachtree Street but insisted
that nobody touch her until the Grady ambulance, with a
doctor in attendance, arrived.

Victims of the Winecoff Hotel fire in which one hundred
people were killed December 7, 1946, were taken first to
Grady. I still remember the pitiful throngs of people gathered
in the morgue in the basement of the old Grady, trying to
identify relatives from shards of bones and poignant chunks
of melted jewelry.

Nothing really reflects Atlanta's growth better than "the
Grady's." Its old building thrust out annexes in all directions
and underground corridors to connect with equally ram-
shackle units across the street. It was crowded, hopelessly

dingy and a mélange of the worst smells of illness, disinfect-
ant and poverty.

On sunny days visitors filled the benches on the sidewalk,
listening sometimes with mystification, to Grady's famous
"talking magnolia tree." A speaker from the hospital public
address system hung from a branch, well-hidden by foliage,
and it was strange and a little fearsome, unless you knew
about it, to hear a voice emanating from the tree shrilly pag-
ing doctors, who might be crossing the street between buildings.

"Saturday night at the Grady" has always been high drama.
Victims from wrecks and shooting matches and cutting
scrapes and drinking sprees are hauled into the emergency
clinic, along with old people, taken mysteriously ill in the
night, and feverish, fretful babies come down with urgent
rashes and croups.

The talking magnolia tree still stands and still speaks
and Saturday nights in the emergency clinic are pretty much
the same. But since 1958, Grady Hospital's building has been
one of the handsomest things on the skyline—a tall clean rectangle of a building which cost $25 million and which gleam-
ingly houses more than a thousand patients (not counting
325 bassinets for new arrivals) and treats half a million out-
patients each year.

Its eighth floor, as warmly and invitingly furnished as a college fraternity house, operates as a psychiatric intensive treatment center, run in conjunction with the State Health Department and Emory. (Emory also has a twenty-bed facility
for nervous and mental disorders and there are four privately
owned and operated institutions in Greater Atlanta for such
treatment.)

Although medical training in Atlanta is centered in Emory and the school accounts for about half of the $10 million spent annually in almost five hundred projects here, there are many other hospitals and groups engaging in research.

Piedmont Hospital, for instance, has an established research department and opportunities for doctors to serve as research fellows after basic house training. There are twenty-five projects ranging from methods of preventing clotting in damaged small blood vessels to new methods of treating obesity now underway.

The Fulton County Health Department conducts field work projects for other health agencies in such varied fields as Staphylococcus infection and ringworm. At Atlanta University, Spelman College and Georgia Tech projects related to temperature stress on blood plasma proteins, parasitic protozoa and space medicine have been going on for some time.

The Atlanta Veterans Administration Hospital carries on extensive research in microbiology, tuberculosis, cancer and hospital infections.

The most far-reaching research work of all probably goes on at the big Communicable Disease Center, national headquarters for the U. S. Public Health Service's work in infectious diseases. Approximately six million dollars a year is spent here on more than two hundred research projects. The center is situated near the Emory University campus in new laboratories and administrative offices, finished in 1960. A great deal of its work never makes the daily newspapers and some projects are so complicated they must make dull reading even for subscribers of the scientific journals.

But to fifteen million leprosy sufferers in Africa and Asia the announcement early in 1963 that a doctor at CDC in

Atlanta had found a way to test antileprosy drugs and vaccines in the laboratory rather than in human patients should have been glad tidings.

Dr. Charles C. Shepard, chief of the special projects unit, virology section, had finally confirmed to his satisfaction finds he made in 1957. Leprosy bacilli would grow on the footpads of white mice.

He chose the feet because they were the coolest part of the mice—and in human beings leprosy bacilli affect the cooler parts of the body, the skin, the mucous membrane and peripheral nervous system. The rear feet were chosen because they are larger and provide more space for cultivation than the front feet. The right rear foot was used simply as a matter of being systematic, Dr. Shepard said.

Since death from leprosy seems a remote prospect to the average American, news of Dr. Shepard's work probably didn't set pulses hammering in the man on the street. But CDC looks ahead. There are only two thousand known cases in this country, but as we draw closer to our neighbors in the tropical countries the development of antileprosy drugs and vaccines grows more important to us.

So it is with much of the research going on in Atlanta today. And Dr. Gilbert, riding into town with his whistle and his quinine more than a century ago, was the beginning of it all.

Atlanta Newspapers—
A Prejudiced View

CHAPTER XI

They say the wife is always the last to know and I never understood better how she, poor wretch, must feel than I did in the spring of 1950. I was practically the last to know about the merger of the two big Atlanta newspapers.

Just as the deceived wife, who finds that her husband is involved with another, must start mentally retracing the path, trying to remember where her attention was when he started these shenanigans, I think back to the merger as somehow coming about because I was bogged down in that elephant idiocy.

It doesn't matter now, of course. The thing is past. The morning Atlanta *Constitution*, founded in 1868 and published by the Howell family since 1876, and the evening Atlanta *Journal*, founded in 1883 and published by the Cox

family of Ohio since 1939, are under one roof and one ownership—Atlanta Newspapers, Inc. And if it was not a love match
but a marriage of convenience with, editorially speaking, separate beds and separate rooms for the partners, it's still a lot
different from the way things were the winter an old elephant
named Alice died at the Atlanta City Zoo.

The two newspapers lived apart and were as hotly competitive as is possible with different deadlines and different press
times. We of the *Constitution* staff had only recently moved
into a new building at the corner of Forsyth and Alabama
Streets (now occupied by the Georgia Power Company) and
were feeling smug, albeit a little homesick for the dingy, cu-
polated old Victorian home across the street where Henry
Grady, Joel Chandler Harris and Frank L. Stanton had
worked. The *Journal* also had new digs—a whole refurbished
office building and, going up cheek by jowl, a new structure
to house its mechanical departments.

There was outwardly nothing to indicate we were about to
be blended.

And then, as I said, that old elephant named Alice died.

I was out of town covering a murder trial at the time and
I paid scant attention to the emotional stories in both papers
about this cataclysmic tragedy at the zoo and the widespread
mourning among kiddies. The jury brought in an acquittal
for the defendant in my murder trial (a state senator) and I
came home to pick up a new assignment.

"This is right down your alley," said Luke Greene, our then
city editor—and I winced, recognizing the preface to a clinker
of a chore.

It was.

"I want you to get us an elephant for the zoo," said Mr. Greene. "You may have noticed the *Journal* has started a campaign for one. So you'll have to get us a bigger and better elephant—and get it faster."

I had indeed noticed that the *Journal* had a campaign going to buy a replacement for Alice. How could I miss with my own children, sharper than a serpent's tooth, demanding dimes to contribute to it through their school? The *Journal*'s elephant drive was surging ahead, no school child left unturned.

For a day or two I followed the same tack, working children's hospitals and orphanages and coming up with a grand total of about $7.82. After about a week I knew I had to find an angel for our elephant campaign and I started casting about for some public-spirited citizen in whose heart there burned—or could be kindled—philanthropy and a tender regard for elephants.

It came to me in the middle of the night: Asa Griggs Candler, Jr.

Mr. Candler, son of the founder of the Coca-Cola Company, was a man who thought so highly of elephants he once maintained a stable of them in the front yard of his home on Briarcliff Road. In fact, he may have been the only man on the continent of North America to plow his kitchen garden with elephants. He had a whole zoo on his grounds, established after his first wife had, on a trip west, expressed a desire to have an antelope for a pet. She found one waiting for her when she got home, the nucleus of a full-scale zoo.

The neighbors complained about every aspect of that zoo, smells, sounds and escapes. Some people had even gone to court about it, among them one badly shaken woman who went out to get in her car one morning and found a fugitive monkey behind the steering wheel. So Mr. Candler had reluctantly given up his menagerie, presenting the whole works to the city, including four elephants—the forerunners of the late lamented Alice. Their names: Coca, Cola, Pause and Refreshes.

I didn't know Mr. Candler, but I was desperate. I put in a call to his public relations expert, a nice young man named Harold Brown. Would Mr. Candler, proven friend of the zoo, care to go for another elephant?

Harold wasn't sure that Mr. Candler would feel like further philanthropy in this direction. Atlanta's zoo was then terribly run down and seedy-looking. His other pachyderm gifts there had not flourished. Pause, Refreshes and Coca had preceded Alice in death. Even multimillionaires aren't eager to throw good elephants after bad.

However, Harold promised to talk to Mr. Candler and call me back. I moped around the office, scrounging a few elephant fund coins where I could—and thinking about Mr. Candler. His public relations, even to my untutored eye, looked a bit frayed and in need of mending. The zoo suits had been followed by a fire in his dry-cleaning establishment, in which hundreds of Atlanta citizens had literally lost the shirts off their backs. And before that could be adjusted Mr. Candler had embarked on a program to take the tombstones out of old Westview Cemetery, which he owned, and make it a modern, parklike burying place with vast sweeps of green lawn, all perpetually cuttable by power mower. The howls of outraged citizens were even then reverberating throughout the Fulton County Courthouse.

Harold Brown called me back. Mr. Candler would see me—

in his office in a vast, windowless building in the middle of Westview Cemetery.

Well, the result of our meeting was, from my point of view, fantastically successful. Mr. Candler, who in his youth had been an African big game hunter in the best Hemingway tradition, would on the following Saturday give a wild-animal party for children in his trophy room in the cemetery. At the height of the party he would unveil a check made payable "To The Children of Atlanta" in the amount of whatever sum would be needed to supplement the lagging *Constitution* elephant fund. In exchange we were to conduct an essay contest, "Why I Would Like to Help Select Coca II," with six schoolchildren winners to fly with Mr. Candler in his private plane into the wilds of darkest New Hampshire to Benson's Wild Animal Farm.

There were minor disparagements. On the very Sunday the *Constitution* triumphantly bannered this story with a picture of Mr. Candler, children and check on the front page, Columnist Doris Lockerman, who had not been apprised of the coup, wrote on an inside page that there were plenty of rich men in Atlanta who could buy an elephant for the zoo but we didn't want that—"we want the elephant to be bought with the pennies of children." And at Sunday School one of my dearest friends remarked churlishly that "*that* Asa Candler" had committed the crowning outrage of his career— "wild-animal party on the hallowed ground of old Westview."

But I weathered them and the most wholesale-entered essay contest I ever saw and one early spring day photographer Marion Johnson and I met Mr. Candler, his press agent, Harold Brown, his son-in-law, Tom Callaway, City Parks Director

George Simon, and six essay winners at the airport to take off for New Hampshire.

Our departure was only slightly clouded by a brief story in the morning paper to the effect that during the night the *Journal* had attended the going-out-of-business sale of a defunct circus in Athens and brought home, under cover of darkness, a moth-eaten little old elephant, to be named "Penny"—for guess whose pennies?

Beating them to their own announcement had taken the zing out of their story, we felt, even if the razzle-dazzle of our elephant hunt had not. And it was a razzle-dazzle hunt, for sure. Mr. Candler was an aviation enthusiast. His harness race track was the site of the Atlanta Airport and he was one of the first businessmen in America to acquire a private plane. So he had a luxury, twenty-passenger plane with two pilots to take us first to Washington, where we were received by his old college classmate, the Veep, Vice-President Alben Barkley. We had a day of sight-seeing by chartered bus and then on to Boston, where another chartered bus picked us up for the trip to New Hampshire and the wild-animal farm.

The essay winners picked an elephant, with only a little prompting from Mr. Candler and me. (He knew quality and I was interested in size.) We flew back to Atlanta and the elephant, dispatched with bands playing and flags flying and a ceremony attended by the Mayor of the town, was to follow us in a heated van with a vet in attendance.

He was due on Saturday, and on Thursday our then managing editor, Lee Rogers (now public relations director for Lockheed) flung another journalistic hand grenade in my direction.

"We should have a parade to welcome our elephant," he said. "Get one up."

It would have been a little silly to protest that I was a reporter and not a promoter since I had already promoted an elephant. So, numbly, not knowing the first thing about it, I set to work and by Friday night I had conned every friend, every acquaintance, every news source at my command into putting something—bands, clowns, tumblers, *anything*— into the parade. As an afterthought I looked around for a parade marshal and Mike Benton, longtime Southeastern Fair impresario and a veteran of many parades, came to my rescue. It was he who mentioned the matter of the police permit.

Police Chief Herbert Jenkins, normally a brave man, blanched in horror.

"Do you realize it's Easter Saturday?" he whispered. "We can't add a parade to that traffic!"

Eventually, of course, the chief relented. And after a bad night, during which I alternately tossed fitfully and phoned the State Patrol to be sure the *Journal* had not hijacked our elephant, we were ready for the arrival of Coca II.

Governor Herman Talmadge was not available for official welcoming but Mayor Hartsfield was, and the First Lady and the little Talmadge sons, Bobby and Gene, were going to meet Coca II in front of the *Constitution* building and give him his "first taste of Georgia peanuts."

The *Journal*'s then city editor, Bob Collins, declined our telegraphed invitation to cover the festivities, but everybody else was there, radio, television, wire services and newsreel.

Our chief, Ralph McGill, emceed the show from the *Constitution* lobby—in front of the gold seal which reads, "Wisdom, Justice, Moderation." At the crucial moment when we hoped the eyes of the world were riveted on our triumph, the little Talmadge boys, their hands loaded with Georgia peanuts, took one look at Coca II and turned tail and ran, howling in terror.

Editor McGill snatched up Gene, the eldest—named for his grandfather, the old governor—spanked him soundly and thrust him back to do his duty.

Beautiful Betty Talmadge was mighty gracious about it when Mr. McGill apologized to her afterward. He didn't know what possessed him to start spanking the child, he confessed ruefully, unless it was reflex action—the old irresistible urge to hit a Talmadge.

I slunk home for a week's vacation. And the very next Saturday our political editor at the time, M. L. St. John, who has since also gone to Lockheed, telephoned to tell me that the Sunday papers were to announce the merger of the *Constitution* with the *Journal*.

"We might not need you any more," he warned me. "We've decided to put all our elephants in one basket."

Time recorded the event another way: Atlanta now has two newspapers, two elephants and one publisher.

When I began this chapter on Atlanta newspapers, friends suggested tactfully that I might have trouble combating a bit of natural bias. After all, a newspaperwoman who thinks journalism is a holy cause and the Atlanta *Constitution* practically its anointed apostle, how could I be sure of giving an objective picture of the field? Was it possible for me to render an impartial judgment between my own *Constitution*, for instance, and those people downstairs on the *Journal*?

Certainly it's possible. I can leave all personal feeling out of this and do a careful, accurate job of factual reporting. In fact, I did—for fifteen of the dullest pages I ever read in my life. I have thrown them in the trash basket. Anybody who wants a good careful, accurate job of factual reporting on this subject can get James Reston or Theodore White. Or, maybe easier, telephone the newspapers' promotion department and request the vital statistics in easy, mimeographed capsule form.

When you get an insider's view, you get feeling—love, loyalty, prejudice, antagonism and maybe a corny kind of special family humor.

So I begin with prejudice.

The *Constitution* is my paper. It's famous, faulty, full of courage and utterly individual. I would have died if I hadn't got a job on it, because even down in South Alabama, where its circulation was, at most, spotty, I was reared to believe that the *Constitution* was the South's greatest newspaper and one of the world's most distinguished, a belief I still hold.

The *Journal* is a good newspaper, lively, aggressive, well written, well edited, with more circulation than the *Constitution* and therefore more advertising linage and more space for news. In the classic words of the prejudiced everywhere, some of my best friends are *Journal* people. This isn't a local situation, of course. Newspaper people always gravitate to other newspaper people, setting aside their professional rivalry after hours to enjoy their common interests. But it may be especially true in Atlanta because so many people have worked on both staffs.

Jack Spalding, editor of the *Journal*, for instance, is closer to many *Constitution* staffers than our own editor, Eugene Patterson, or even our publisher, Mr. McGill, from having

worked at the next desk, shared telephones and coffee breaks
and beefs about assignments. He started as a reporter on the
Constitution, went away to the United Press and the World
War II Navy, and returned to the *Journal*. The *Constitution*
lured him back to write editorials and a sharp, literate edito-
rial-page column. He married the prettiest courthouse reporter
we ever had, the former Anne Gowen, and in 1957 left us
again—this time to be editor of the *Journal*.

His *Constitution* friends, dazzled by the promotion, overlooked the disloyalty implicit in his desertion. As a newsroom
slave, Spalding had been a fairly rare animal—a reporter with
money in his pocket. His family were old settlers, wealthy, socially prominent and influential. His father, Hughes Spalding,
a corporation lawyer with the face of an old eagle, has been a
power in nearly every good cause in Atlanta for more than
half a century, most notably perhaps the Roman Catholic
Church, in which he is a Papal Privy Chamberlain of Cape
and Sword.

The fact that Jack considered working for a newspaper more
interesting and of more urgent importance than a berth in a
family enterprise or than selling stocks and bonds or running
a fruit plantation in South America, both of which he tried,
would have helped us forgive his money and membership in
the Piedmont Driving Club, if we ever had to. Happily, it
didn't come up. The personality of the man himself spared
us this form of inverted snobbery. He was a diligent reporter,
he is a gifted and amusing writer and an enormously kind,
generous friend who hides his personal good works and affection back of a prickly pear hedge of humor, so spiky it keeps
all egos, including his own, well deflated.

The *Journal* staff is studded with people for whom I have

warm personal as well as professional regard—Associate Editor Luke Greene, a *Constitution* alumnus mentioned earlier as the author of the elephant assignment; Frank Daniel, reporter-columnist oft quoted here and a gentleman of taste and erudition; Charlie Pou, the political editor and a low-key, deadpan humorist whose mumbled witticisms have brightened many an otherwise dull assignment for me. (His wife is Genevieve Holden, the murder mystery writer.) Pat Watters, who gave up city editing to write a column and edit the book page, brought fresh readability to the editorial page, where for so many years the brightest star has been Ernest Rogers, the cheerful fellow on crutches, who was known as "The Mayor of Peachtree Street," now in semiretirement.

Margaret Shannon, the *Journal*'s Washington correspondent, is probably one of the ablest reporters in the country. Furman Bisher, who left the *Constitution* to take the post of *Journal* sports editor when the late nationally renowned Ed Danforth retired, is himself a writer enjoyed and acclaimed in books and magazine pieces beyond his daily column. Edith Hills Coogler, women's editor, uses a typewriter ribbon inked with mirth and vinegar and she never wrote a dull or commonplace line in her life, even about dull and commonplace subjects. Hugh Park's "Around Town" column and the little Page One paragraphs called "Street Scene," which he writes or edits, are highly local, unfailingly interesting.

There's no point in attempting to call the roll here, for it is a big, brisk staff of smart, talented men and women, many of them old-timers who have seen service on both papers, many of them youngsters.

Of course, back in 1950 the *Journal* staff was as apprehensive about the merger as we were. Politicians shouted "Monopoly!" Advertisers expected the worst, although there are about twenty other papers—one daily, the Marietta *Journal,* the others weeklies—in the Atlanta area. Reporters and editors on both sides of the viaduct were certain some of us wouldn't, as Saint had said, "be needed any more."

Many people at the *Journal* had gone through a similar experience in 1939. The day of the *Gone With the Wind* première, with the whole town in carnival mood, they had learned that the *Journal* and its radio station, WSB, had been sold, and so had the other afternoon paper, William Randolph Hearst's Atlanta *Georgian.* The buyer was the head of the Cox chain, James M. Cox, the colorful former Governor of Ohio, who with Franklin D. Roosevelt as his teammate had run against Warren G. Harding for President in 1920.

The *Journal* had fared fine under the new ownership, but the *Georgian* had folded and its editors and reporters scattered. Some, of course, found a berth on the *Journal,* some on the *Constitution,* but many had to move on to other cities or quit the newspaper business altogether.

Nobody at the *Constitution,* except possibly one or two in the highest echelon, had ever dreamed that Major Clark Howell, whose father and grandfather had preceded him at its helm, would ever relinquish the famous old paper. To sell out was crushing enough, but this was selling out to the enemy. We felt certain we would be gobbled up, absorbed, lose our identity completely. We heard all kinds of sinister things about the way they ran the *Journal.*

We heard it was one of those efficient, clean-desk operations. They were understood to pay reporters more, but they were picky about hours and expense accounts. On the *Constitution* before we moved into our new building we had to share desks and sometimes wait in line for a typewriter. And there was a *Constitution* reporter of legend who had kept a U-Drive-It and had drawn expense money for weeks on a voucher which said succinctly: "Covering floods in Alabama." I don't know when, if ever, the bookkeeping department learned that this was during a season of prolonged drouth in our neighboring state.

The *Journal* rode buses on assignment. We grandly took taxis, signing the meter tickets. You had to have a pass to get in the *Journal* building at night. The *Constitution* stairway was a sort of ascending flophouse for old newsies and visiting bums and drunks who slept there out of the cold in winter. (A subscriber once complained to Major Howell that he found a bedbug in his morning paper and the Mayor is said to have replied cheerfully, "What did you expect for a nickel?")

Taking whiskey into the *Journal* building was a firing offense. To old hands on the *Constitution* a few drinks and a game of poker around the copy desk after the paper was put to bed came under the head of wholesome employee recreation. The *Journal* was said to have a splendid well-run reference department with complete clip files, microfilm machines and a professional librarian in charge. The *Constitution* had a file room, presided over part time by a kid who was going to Tech, and when you were looking for a picture or a clipping you sometimes blundered into a filing cabinet of empty liquor bottles and old sandwich crusts.

The *Journal* had a Sunday Magazine supplement, precisely and exquisitely produced for more than forty years under the direction of Angus Perkerson (now retired and succeeded by George Hatcher). The *Constitution* was later to contribute the eminent Kenneth Rogers to head the magazine's photographic department, but at that time our Sunday supplement consisted of a couple of feature pages put together by a brilliant, erratic old Hearst man who bragged that he had been fired from nearly every paper in the country "but never for incompetence, always for drinking."

The *Constitution*'s business operation was something out of a Dickens novel, a sleeve garter and alpaca vest thing run by a kindly old gentleman who mended his glasses with twine, devoted his lunch hours to playing pinochle down at the fire station and, as awed observers later noted, "spent a dollar to save a dime any day." The *Constitution*'s circulation department was run by a union so exclusive it was easier for a newcomer to town to get in the Piedmont Driving Club than to get a subscription to the paper.

What then, you may wonder, did the *Constitution* have to bring to this merger?

It had color. It drew characters. Being in that newsroom was so much fun staff members hung around on their own time— no time-and-a-half overtime consideration. I remember one night during the war a young soldier and his girl wandered in asking how they could get married in a hurry before he was shipped overseas. They were strangers in town and they had practically no money. We didn't have any money either but we had connections. We whipped them up a newsroom wedding in nothing flat. The late City Recorder Luke Arnold was rounded up to officiate, the famous Negro accordionist Graham Jackson was recruited to play the wedding march. The city editor gave the bride away, the copy desk served as groomsmen, the church editor as maid of honor. We took up a collection and hired them a hotel room for their honeymoon and then, full of sentiment and file room punch, we danced dreamily to accordion music.

Schoolchildren tours still came to Atlanta newspapers, sedately conducted by young women from the promotion department. But the *Constitution* of the old days used to give them a real show. When we heard them coming, the boys used to scramble for hats to set on the back of their heads, stick press cards in the bands and rend the air with cries of "Flash!" and "Stop the press!" And pint-sized Lee Fuhrman, then city editor, was never too busy to respond royally, "Get me Joe Stalin on the phone! Get me Eleanor Roosevelt!"

Writers and reporters, photographers and artists seem to have flourished in this easy, unregimented atmosphere. Three times the *Constitution* has won Pulitzer prizes—once in 1931 for Herman Hancock's reporting of city hall graft, in 1958 for Ralph McGill's editorials and in 1959 for Jack Nelson's exposé of conditions at the state mental hospital. Even now the staff bristles with Nieman fellows—Nelson, who recently co-authored with Gene Roberts, Jr., of the Raleigh *Times Observer* a penetrating analysis of the textbook crisis, *The Censors and the Schools*; the present political editor, Reg Murphy; Marvin Wall, editorial writer and columnist; and Bruce Galphin, a young student of race relations.

It even holds, despite his success in a worldwide vineyard, such people as Harold H. Martin. Harold is a *Constitution* reporter-columnist whose stories from the Pacific as a Marine combat correspondent during World War II brought him to the attention of the *Saturday Evening Post*. He joined the *Post* staff after the war as a roaming editor, covering assignments in far corners of the world, but, alone among *Post* people, he has kept his old job, too. Thrice a week his columns of humor and warmth appear on the *Constitution* editorial page. Some of these columns were compiled a few years back in the highly successful book, *Father's Day Comes Once a Year, and Then It Always Rains.*

Looking back, it's funny that in 1950 we of the *Constitution* didn't dream that the new owners really knew or valued the odd, obstreperous, perversely accomplished crew at the *Constitution.* Merger, we said, ha. More likely a submerger.

Two people were soon to learn better.

Ralph McGill, the stocky, perpetually worried-looking man who had risen from the ranks as a sportswriter to become one of the country's more famous editors, and his next in command, Jack Tarver, were summoned to Miami to talk with Governor Cox. They came away awestruck.

The old gentleman knew a great deal about the operation of both papers, including the names and comparative talents of minor editors and writers. He wanted the combined Sunday paper to be a blending of the best of each. He asked Tarver to take a hand in directing the operation. As for McGill, he was a long-time McGill fan, and he had but one order for him—the only one, Mr. McGill says, the old Governor gave him from that day until his death at the age of eighty-seven in 1957. He wanted the McGill column to be moved from the editoral page to column one, page one.

For Jack Tarver, thirty-three years old and just home from a year spent in South America on a Fulbright fellowship, the merger meant new direction to a career with which he was getting restless and dissatisfied. It meant use for hitherto unused talents.

Tarver was to drop the highly successful editorial page column which he wrote for the *Constitution* and which was being syndicated in thirty-four other newspapers, and join George C. Biggers, president of the new combine, in the task of management.

Some readers are still unreconciled to that change, remembering with a feeling of real loss the lethally amusing Tarverisms. A brief column, seldom running more than half a dozen paragraphs, it commented on the political and social scene with such humor that, as one victim pointed out, "You die laughing before you even notice you've been fatally harpooned."

Tarver made the change, not only cheerfully but with a sense of larger destiny, looking on it as an opportunity, among other things, to free the *Constitution* from business problems which had bedeviled its old-fashioned management, and to bolster its editorial independence. He liked both George Biggers and Governor Cox and he liked seeing his friend, mentor and hero, McGill, reaching a wider audience.

"Somebody has to steady the soapbox," he remarked with characteristic irreverence.

Seven years later, when Mr. Biggers retired and moved to Florida, where he died in the spring of 1963, Tarver was to succeed him as president of Atlanta Newspapers, Inc., and a bit later in 1958 he was named executive vice-president of the Cox owned Miami *News*.

Jack has an answer for all the erstwhile fellow toilers in the dirty, crowded old *Constitution* newsroom when they marvel that the moon-faced, bespectacled young man who used to hunch over his typewriter, agonizingly sweating out humor in a cubbyhole back of the elevator, knows how to run this mammoth enterprise.

"Hell, I ran a country weekly, didn't I?" he asks, recalling his first job in Lyons, Georgia, and poking a crooked forefinger at you by way of illustration. "I bet I'm the only metropolitan publisher in the country who ever caught a hand in a flatbed press."

If Tarver "steadies the soapbox"—and both present editors of Atlanta newspapers affirm that he does, giving them not only freedom but freedom to disagree with him and with each other—a great deal of credit goes to Ralph McGill.

McGill, who moved up to publisher of the *Constitution* in 1960 after more than thirty years with the paper, has justified and glorified the use of the editorial soapbox.

The *Constitution* was born in crisis and named in optimism. Founded in 1868 when carpetbag rule harassed Georgia, the paper's name was suggested by President Andrew Johnson as appropriate for a newspaper seeking to restore constitutional government to the South. Although he has been with it not quite a third of its life, the name of Ralph McGill has become synonymous with that of the paper. There are places in the world, mostly those accessible only by camelback, where Atlanta, even America, is known chiefly because it is the home of the *Constitution*'s Ralph McGill.

Sometimes he is referred to as the conscience of the South, and in Atlanta his function is frequently summed up in the words of one subscriber who said simply, "He does my thinking for me."

An east Tennessean, a World War I Marine and a near-graduate of Vanderbilt University (he was kicked out before graduation for something he wrote in the campus humor mag-

7   Scene from the Cyclorama.

8 Pouring ingots
at a steel plant.

9 A bit of the vast Lake Chatuge in the North Georgia mountains.

10   Dogwood season.

11   One of the reasons Georgia is a great medical center.

12   Hitting the road to town on Saturday.

azine), McGill came to the *Constitution* in 1929 to write sports. He happened to be in Cuba on vacation when the 1933 revolution broke out and he dropped his vacation to cover the revolution. In 1938 his interest in farm tenancy problems won him a Rosenwald Foundation fellowship to study agricultural co-ops and marketing conditions in Scandinavia, so he happened to be on hand as Hitler prepared to invade Austria. He abandoned his peacetime studies, rushed to Austria and covered the opening phase of the second great war. He came home in 1939 to find he had been promoted from sports editor to executive editor. Three years later he became editor-in-chief.

McGill fought the Ku Klux Klan in the years when it still retained so much power that most southern politicians gave it acceptance through their silence, if they were not actually members of it. He championed the case of Negro rights before "integration" was more than a crossword puzzle type word. As Harry Ashmore, former editor of the Arkansas *Gazette*, once said of him, "McGill had guts when it wasn't easy to have guts."

Love of his region has never blinded him to its faults nor kept him silent. He goes along with the late "Marse" Henry Watterson of Louisville, who contended in a bit of poesy:

> *Things have come to a hell of a pass*
> *When a man can't flog his own jackass.*

He has won a staggering number of honors and awards. It's a routine day for him to dash off his column and catch a plane somewhere to accept a new honorary degree or plaque, prize or citation. He has been adviser to four Presidents. (He is currently a member of the President's Advisory Commit-

tee on Labor-Management Policy and the Advisory Committee of the Arms Control and Disarmament Agency.) His lat-
est book, *The South and the Southerner*, a luminous, eyewitness account of stirring days in his region's life and times,
won the Atlantic Non-Fiction Award.

Around his own shop his staff is proud of him but not
reverent. Poking fun at his foibles and arguing with his views
are allowable because McGill treats himself the same, regard-
ing himself as a fairly ridiculous fellow, fumbling for the
truth, humble before the great mystery of life itself, eternally
subject to error.

He not only permits disagreement from his aides, he en-
courages it. An ardent Democrat and a wholehearted and enthusiastic supporter of Franklin D. Roosevelt, Adlai Stevenson and John F. Kennedy, he hired some years ago a young
man from Savannah who was known to have Republican
leanings and who was suspected of being, in the McGill
phrase, "a moss-back reactionary." The young man, William
H. Fields, advanced rapidly from the post of editorial assistant to associate editor and managing editor, not because he
tactfully suppressed views counter to those of his boss but
because he advanced them boldly and argued them with a
sharp and caustic intelligence which delighted McGill.

This is in the *Constitution* tradition. The Confederate captain, Evan P. Howell, allowed McGill's illustrious predecessor,
Henry W. Grady, the same freedom. Editor Grady fought
for prohibition while Captain Howell, the publisher, opposed
it. Grady was active in the dry camp, Captain Howell was
active in the wet camp and neither side was stinted on space
in the pages of the *Constitution*. Captain Howell's son, the
present Major Clark Howell, Jr., former publisher, now vice-

chairman of the board and a major stockholder, continued the policy which McGill once described as "hiring writers and letting them write."

McGill himself hasn't actively directed writing and editing by other people around the *Constitution* for some time. He has always shucked executive problems where he could, preferring to be out in the thick of things himself, covering wars and politics. In 1960 when he moved up to publisher he was succeeded by another writing, reporting editor of the Grady stripe, a young South Georgian named Eugene Patterson.

Gene Patterson, now thirty-nine, like many of us grew up with an exalted regard for the old *Constitution*. He admired the paper and McGill from afar—passing the building on trips to Atlanta from his home in Adel, Georgia, but too shy to walk in and apply for a job. It wasn't until 1947 when as a twenty-three-year-old lieutenant in the peacetime Army he grew dissatisfied with military life and decided to try newspapering. He got out of the Army at Camp Hood, Texas, and got a job on a paper in Temple, Texas, where, he later said, "I had three very swift months, making a hell of a mess of everything I did and enjoying it immensely."

Patterson moved from Texas closer home, to the Macon (Georgia) *Telegraph*, and then he went with the United Press, first to Columbia, South Carolina, where he met and married a newspaperwoman, the former Sue Carter, then to New York and finally to London. In London it was Gene's job as a wire service executive in 1953 to meet and help entertain a visiting publisher and his wife, Mr. and Mrs. George Biggers of Atlanta.

Some months later, weary of living abroad and the impersonality of wire service work, Patterson started thinking about

a job back in Georgia. He wrote Mr. Biggers and asked him if
he knew of anything. To his surprise Mr. Biggers invited him
to come to Atlanta to begin as an editorial writer on the
Journal, with a view to "working out something else."

The first "something else" was executive editor of both papers. And then McGill, nearing sixty-five, moved up to publisher, and the job Gene regarded as "the greatest honor available to any newspaperman in the country," being editor of the
Constitution, was his.

Gene says he took it "in fear and trembling" and he's still
boyishly impressed by it, despite the verve and authority his
writing has given the editorial page and his fresh and confident direction of the news operation. As a relative newcomer
to the papers, Patterson may view them with more objectivity
than most of us.

He believes that out of the merger both papers got an auton-
omy unknown to most group ownerships. He credits Mr. Biggers with pulling the best men from both papers for key jobs,
a policy Jack Tarver has continued.

"They hire you because they know what you can do and
then they don't stand and look over your shoulder," Patterson
said. "You can say whatever you please and they have more
respect for you than if you hedge and try to please."

Recently Patterson sat in his office on the fifth floor of the
newspapers' 10 Forsyth Street Building (the *Journal* editorial
and news departments are on the fourth floor) and realized
that most of the old fights, from Henry Grady's days up
through McGill's battles against demagoguery and the county
unit system, had been won.

What's ahead?

He thinks first education and then industrial development

—not "the minimum wage, linthead labor, sewing machine plant" type of industry but the kind which demands skilled, educated labor and pays high wages, the kind which will utilize the scientific, space age research at our university centers.

"Educate people and give them decent pay and the cultural level will come up," Editor Patterson says. "Georgians are sturdy characters, pure granite when they're wrong, and pure granite when they're right. Education must be our top priority fight for the future. We have to teach our people to live up to their raising."

Well, Mr. Asa Candler is dead now, and his home where Atlanta elephants got their start is now a state hospital for the treatment of alcoholism—a poetic use of an estate that soft drink built. There's a whole new zoo at Grant Park and a new cat house as well as a new elephant house. I haven't checked on Coca II lately, but then I've been busy and it's possible she had nothing to do with the destiny of Atlanta newspapers after all.

"Ain't That a Van Gogh?"

CHAPTER XII

When Chief Justice Earl Warren of the U. S. Supreme Court came to Atlanta to make a speech at Georgia Tech in February 1963, there was a minor movement among members of the local John Birch Society to make him feel unwelcome. Signs saying, "Impeach Earl Warren," were hoisted in a few places and there were threats of an airport demonstration to express displeasure at his desegregation decision.

Mayor Ivan Allen, unwilling to have such a prominent guest go away with the feeling that our town was inhospitable, promptly alerted the police force and then he himself met Mr. Justice Warren's plane and cordially but stubbornly stuck to him closer than a brother for the duration of his visit.

When the visit ended without incident, the New York *Times*'s local man, Claude Sitton, asked a police official if safeguarding the chief justice had been much of a job.

"Oh, hell no," the officer said easily. "We got more men on Whistler's Mother than we had on *him!*"

Whatever the Police Department's reasoning, the emphasis was exactly right. The preponderance of Atlanta's population was a great deal more interested in art than it was in a grudge session with Chief Justice Earl Warren.

In fact, even at that moment throngs which were in a few weeks to total more than 118,000 people were filing through the Atlanta Art Association's McBurney Hall to take a look at James McNeill Whistler's maternal parent and a French traveling companion, "The Penitent St. Mary Magdalene" by Georges de la Tour, who had arrived in Atlanta from the Louvre a couple of days before the Chief Justice.

The presence of these two famous paintings in Atlanta's unpretentious, unspectacular museum was, in a way, evidence that the city is, as one artist happily phrased it, "ripping into a cultural renaissance that won't wait."

They were on loan from the French Government, in tribute to 122 Atlantans who were killed in a jetliner which crashed and burned on takeoff from Orly Airport in France the morning of June 3, 1962. These people, leaders in Atlanta's social, civic and artistic life, were homeward bound after touring European art centers on a trip sponsored by the Atlanta Art Association. The crash was one of the worst disasters in history and a stunning blow to our town, where there were few people who did not have ties of friendship, kinship or business with one or more of the victims.

For months there were recurring reminders of the tragedy.

Mayor Allen went to Paris to investigate the crash and to make arrangements for the return of the few sad remnants of the bodies and the belongings of the people who had been on the holiday. There were memorial services as bodies were identified and brought home and then the wrenching practical concerns—auctions of homes and furnishings of couples on the plane, an embarrassed inquiry from a vet about what to do with the pets he had been boarding for several of the travelers, a notice in the personal column on the society page that a family of children, orphaned by the crash, were moving away to live with relatives.

The French Ambassador in Washington, His Excellency, Hervé Alphand, announced that his government wished to send pictures from the Louvre—a token of friendship by which "France expresses her sympathy toward a city whose artistic and intellectual élite suffered severe losses in a plane accident at Orly."

Out of the grief and loss, however, Atlanta which years ago took the phoenix bird of mythology as her symbol, found a way to build once more on disaster. It decided to build a new and bigger art school as a memorial to those who died.

The Art Association had already hired a team of New York educational consultants to make a study of its present school and museum. The report of the experts was in hand awaiting action when the trip to Europe was organized. Among the people on that fateful trip was Del R. Paige, president of the Art Association, and Mrs. Paige. James V. Carmichael, chairman of the board of trustees, became Mr. Paige's successor, and he led a movement to "create a living, working, producing and teaching memorial to the memory of these members . . . a new Atlanta School of Art."

The campaign for $1.5 million to build the school was officially launched the bright windy Sunday afternoon in February when a thousand Atlantans gathered on the museum lawn on Peachtree Street to hear the Third Army Band play, to see the French tricolor hoisted beside the American flag and to cheer as Ambassador Alphand cut the ribbons across the door leading to Whistler's Mother and Mary Magdalene.

Atlanta has had an art school and a museum since 1927, housed at first in the old home of Mrs. J. M. High, whose family department store once flourished on Whitehall Street. They grew to take in neighboring homes on both sides, and the school, swelled by veterans after World War II, spread to barracks-like temporary buildings in the backyard. A small but fervent group of prominent Atlantans worked diligently through the years in support of the museum and a small but respectable collection of pictures was gradually assembled, including one of the assortments bestowed on several American cities by the family of Samuel H. Kress, the dime-store king.

But within less than a year after the crash, several important additions took up their residence on Peachtree Street. Some were gifts from the estates of the victims of the crash, many of whom were collectors, some were gifts given in memory of one or more of the travelers. The most valuable new picture, given anonymously as a memorial to the lost members of the Art Association, was a $65,000 painting called "Veronica's Veil," an interpretation of a miracle, by the seventeenth-century Spanish artist Francisco de Zubarán.

The museum collection covers many art styles and spans centuries. In its Kress collection there's Giovanni Bellini's "Madonna and Child," nearly five hundred years old and valued at $100,000. There's a sixteenth-century Tintoretto, "Christ and the Adulteress," valued at $56,000; a Monet, "Houses of Parliament," obtained a few years ago from a New York gallery and now valued at $35,000; and a scattering of small works by more recent greats such as Picasso, Chagall, Dufy, Léger, Renoir and Vlaminck. Long before the French Government's expression of friendship in the loan of Whistler's Mother, a friend of the association had donated nine etchings by Whistler, which hang in the upper gallery.

Art Association officials have no illusions about being able to cop enough of the world's treasures to compete for attention with the nation's already outstanding museums. They hope merely to be good enough and discriminating enough to attract an occasional gift when something notable goes on the market and to team up with other southern cities to bring in exhibits from the great collections of the world. They have hired a new director, Dr. Wilhelmus B. Bryan, a knowledgeable art educator who had reached the age of retirement as director of the Minneapolis School of Art, and felt that he had energy and drive left over to expend in guiding Atlanta toward a real art center. Dr. Reginald Poland, who had long directed the museum here, asked for retirement.

The emphasis in the new art center is to be on the school, already an accredited, degree-awarding college, but cramped in quarters and curriculum. In the new building they hope to have room for three hundred students, instead of the present one hundred and twenty-five and courses to fit commercial-minded artists for jobs in new industries which keep coming to town, as well as the old classic degree subjects.

To Atlanta artists the speed with which art with a capital "A" has acquired social status in our town is a delicious phenomenon. It has always been supported by prominent, well-to-do citizens, as witness the Peachtree Street homes given to the Association, but in recent years it has moved from the exclusive province of what one flippant fellow with paint on his hands called "old ladies with old money" to high fashion.

"I think it's cute that some of these girls who don't know a Caravaggio from a cookstove are breaking their necks to serve as high priestess to the arts," a woman painter in dirty tennis shoes remarked. "I'm not knocking it, understand. We don't have to have the same reasons for getting into things. If they're willing to work like dogs for a museum and a school just to be chic, who am I to tell them they gotta *care* too?"

One good thing about the Art Association is that it has work for all eager hands, whether they are scented with turpentine or Chanel No. 5. Those erstwhile strongholds of the stylish, the Music Club and the opera, are so handsomely supported and so successful they're almost closed corporations. But the Art Association is a pulsing, pushing enterprise with something going on all the time.

Coveys of volunteers attend docent classes to prepare themselves to steer visitors through the museum. Some run the "BBB Shop" (Browse, Borrow and Buy) and do a living business besides in prints and souvenirs, proceeds going to the Association. (Mrs. Frank Ferst, Atlanta's Woman of the Year in Arts for 1962, won the honor for her espousal of the BBB Shop and is such an enthusiastic patron herself even the ceiling of her bathroom is hung with paintings.)

There are period-costume shows and an annual flea market, an elegant antique collectors' show, old movies, foreign movies, Sunday afternoon concerts in the Walter Hill Auditorium, a part of the museum, and the Coach House in the backyard. The Coach House is a notable Atlanta luncheon spot—really a coach house, spruced up and decorated, connected with the rest of the Art Association complex by a walled garden in which only white flowers bloom and a series of terraces and patios, a couple of which are used for lunching. The herb garden and back windows of the Coach House look out on another Art Association project, which is of special interest to architects, interior decorators and gardeners. This is Thornton House, a 1780 vintage Georgia country house, which was moved to Atlanta from Union Point, Georgia, and restored at great expense because it is considered to be an architectural gem of its period.

Of "noggin'" construction with giant double chimneys at the ends and clapboard walls, which were painted a putty color and trimmed with blue shutters, the old house presents an example of social history, garden planning and the building and decorating abilities of a generation of Georgia pioneers. It is open Mondays through Fridays from noon to 3 PM and on Sunday from 2 to 5 PM—one dollar for adults, fifty cents for children.

Another project which contributes to the teeming crowds around the Art Association is the Cherokee Garden Club's annual "Christmas Trees Around the World." The garden club members work for months planning, buying in Europe or making the fixings for a dozen fascinating Yule trees, which are decked early in December and displayed in the museum, proceeds again going to the Art Association. (Atlanta business firms benevolently take turns footing the bills for the trees—not a piddling sum either, but running into several thousand dollars.)

The "art-is-smart" attitude is not the only evidence of an artistic renaissance in Atlanta, however. The ten-day art festival which each May draws an estimated 175,000 people to

Piedmont Park is proof that all kinds of people—and their babies and their dogs—like to look at pictures. Look, and as one of the founders, interior decorator Carolyn Becknell, is wont to crow: "Look, like, buy and take home—like peanuts and hams and taters!"

Miss Becknell insists that the outdoor art festival was, like anesthesia in Dr. Crawford W. Long's day, "on the verge of discovery by everybody" when she and a group of Buckhead neighbors launched it in 1954.

"We were just ten minutes earlier than another group and they later joined us," she explains. At that time she and a landscape architect named Ed Dougherty shared office space in a Buckhead store building and their next-door neighbors were two ceramics teachers, Judy Felton and Olga Heatley. The teachers were planning to exhibit the works of their pupils in a backyard show and Miss Becknell and Mr. Dougherty suggested that they fling in a few pictures.

In a twinkling it had turned into a neighborhood party with pictures and pots and all kinds of crafts represented, a borrowed hi-fi set pouring music out of the bamboo hedge and customers fighting to plunk out more than one thousand dollars for their wares. Next year the foursome, joined by other artists who had the same idea, moved to Piedmont Park.

"We were lucky the city let us in," Carolyn now says. "Every spring there are medicine shows and itinerant preachers dying to pitch their tents in Piedmont Park and the city turns them down, but they let us in and it's terrific. Carnival, festival, fun. We took art out of the mausoleum and had this fool thing in the park and people were ready for it, hungry for it."

The Piedmont show is a free-for-all, for exhibitors as well as viewers. Anybody who has something he made that he wants to show can get in, with but two exceptions:

"No number paintings and no real *nude* nudes," Miss Becknell specifies.

All the crafts are represented—pottery, weaving, jewelry making, wood carving, stained glass, landscape architecture. Local authors are even invited to display and sell their books. The performing arts join up. The Atlanta Symphony sends musicians. So does the Third Army Band, the Atlanta Pops Orchestra, the Emory University Glee Club. The Atlanta Civic Ballet and the Southern Ballet companies send dancers. The theater groups do Shakespeare readings and little plays.

"Once we tried some pretty tense drama," Carolyn recalls. "But outside it's hard for actors to sustain their moods when they have competition from birds in the trees, dogs barking, baseball practice and traffic officers yelling, 'Move along, lady!' So now we keep it light."

The crowds come in blue jeans and pedal pushers, T-shirts and shorts. Youngsters leave the baseball diamond and come to look. One even went home and brought a picture of his own to hang, much to the disgust of his team.

The quality of the show runs from excellent to terrible, but it has stimulated a year-round interest in looking at and buying pictures. As a result, galleries have sprung up all over town. For a long time the only place to buy pictures was at the department stores. A combine of artists called Artists Associates hired an empty store and opened a gallery on West Peachtree Street. Others like Judy Alexander's excellent New Arts Gallery followed to give space to the locals and to bring in many good outside artists.

"Now," says Miss Becknell, "there's one under every flat rock. Anybody who runs a laundry and a bookshop has a gallery on top of that. It's wonderful. Open a door by mistake and, pardon me, it's an art gallery!"

Fulton County schools, under the direction of Miss Emily Rose Wood, have been taking pictures to the rural reaches of the county for a long time. Art travels with the bookmobiles.

A new librarian confessed that at first she thought instruction in art was falling on fallow ground in some of the poorer sections. But she was unloading prints at a country school one day, she said, when a barefoot, overall-clad first grader wandered in and watched her with bright-eyed curiosity. Finally he spoke up.

"Ain't that a Van Gogh?" he asked.

"His knowledge of grammar might have been shaky," the librarian said, "but his knowledge of art was right on the button!"

Atlanta has a growing community of artists, a dozen of whom have received national recognition. Few of them make a living with their pictures or their sculpture, and they work at other jobs for bread and butter and paint or sculpt in hours gouged out of regular workdays. Many teach at the Art School, Emory, Tech, Oglethorpe, Agnes Scott College. Some are architects, some commercial artists.

To stimulate and reward producing artists, two jury shows are held in Atlanta each year—the Southeastern Art Exhibit with a purchase prize of one thousand dollars and Mead Paper Company's "Painting of the Year" contest with a hefty cash prize. The Southeastern, sponsored for years by the department store, Davison-Paxon, always moves from the Art

Association, where it is originally shown, to Peachtree Street, to the show windows of the big store where it is a real traffic stopper.

To add atmosphere, art students don berets and smocks, set up their easels on the sidewalk and paint, if they can, with the crowds jostling their elbows. If they can't, they hand out programs and answer questions about the pictures.

The Atlanta Symphony Orchestra is a force in Atlanta's cultural life which I have followed with enthusiasm since its founding as a youth orchestra in 1945. It has been a fully professional orchestra since 1951 with a budget of over $300,000, which puts it in the top twenty-five symphony orchestras in the country. It is able to attract such guest artists as Glenn Gould, Nathan Milstein and Van Cliburn. The local musicians who make up the orchestra, like painters, frequently support their families by teaching or holding down other jobs, but they came to Atlanta, many of them, because they wanted an opportunity to play with a symphony orchestra. (Martin Sauser, the concertmaster, is an insurance executive; Karl Bevins, clarinetist, is the city traffic engineer.)

Led by its ebullient founder-conductor, Henry Sopkin, the Atlanta Symphony has a flair for the warmhearted and the imaginative. It was one of the first orchestras in the country to give concerts for little children of toddler age. A couple of years ago when Georgia acquired a new state song (words by the late poet laureate, Ollie Reeves, music by Atlantan Frank Black, former conductor of the NBC Symphony Orchestra) Conductor Sopkin and his merry band borrowed Trinity Methodist Church, a block from the capitol, and gave a lunch-hour concert for the legislature.

One of the happiest performances I ever attended was within the walls of Atlanta Penitentiary. The prisoners decked the stage with flowers, spelling out in garlands of roses and fern, "Welcome Atlanta Symphony." The prison bakeshop turned out a monumental cake with the same sentiment in towering icing letters. The audience, Mr. Sopkin said later, was the most attentive and the most appreciative he ever had.

In the middle of an ovation our photographer, Hugh Stovall, asked one rapturously applauding prisoner if he minded if we took his picture for the paper.

"Hell, no!" said the grinning, clapping con. "Why should I mind? It's already in every post office in America!"

These things have endeared the Symphony to Atlantans to the extent that they support the orchestra's twenty-two-week season with their attendance, if not with vast amounts of cash.

There is a seventy-eight-year-old woman who lets neither sleet, snow, dark of night nor rheumatism keep her from performances. She catches a bus to town from far out Peachtree Road, alights at Broad and Walton Streets, and hikes the other six or eight blocks to the Municipal Auditorium to sit in a balcony seat, which costs sixty-two cents on a season ticket basis.

There's a group of young couples who meet for dinner at the Piedmont Driving Club on concert night, leave their cars and board a chartered bus for the auditorium. The cost of the entire evening, arranged for on a package basis, is three dollars per person.

Usually when the season opens the members of the Atlanta Symphony Guild strive for a gala look with formal dress and champagne punch served at intermission. But most nights the Symphony is only a medium dress-up affair, attracting a predominantly youthful and musically astute audience.

However, a Symphony Guild member reports that there is one faithful dowager who had for years occupied the same orchestra seat and observed with growing discontent Conductor Sopkin's preoccupation with guest soloists.

She finally spoke out when Risë Stevens came to town to sing with the orchestra and Maestro Sopkin's attention, as usual, seemed fixed on the shapely singer's chest.

"It does look to me like Henry Sopkin could keep his eyes on the orchestra—at least when he's at work!" she sputtered.

The convulsed Symphony Guilder did her best to explain that Mr. Sopkin enjoys a unique reputation among singers for the care with which he reins in the orchestra to show off the vocalist's best talent. For this reason many big-name concert stars are pleased to come to Atlanta to sing with the Symphony.

"It's not bosoms he's watching, ma'am, it's breathing," the Guild member summed up.

The written word is both an artistic endeavor and an industry in Atlanta, a cultural achievement and a cult. Since "that little Mitchell girl" achieved such phenomenal success, everybody who could scratch up a few Blue Horse tablets and pencil lead to apply thereon has bombarded New York editors and publishers with their prose. Those who are not bold enough to send off their works stow them away in bureau drawers against the time when some hopeful young editor, dreaming of another GWTW, comes to town on a manuscript foraging expedition.

An impressive number of locals have made it, some just

barely, some with plodding, potboiler regularity, some with one-time-and-one-time-only flash and fire.

In the '20s and '30s, Atlanta had not reached its status as a literary watering hole in H. L. Mencken's *Sahara of the Bozart*. It's true a flapper named Frances Newman had startled everybody with a couple of racy novels, one of which had the provocative title, *Dead Lovers Are Faithful Lovers*. Medora Field Perkerson sold a mystery, *Who Killed Aunt Maggie?* both to a publisher and to the movies and went off to Hollywood to help them produce it. She later wrote another one which also went into the movies, *Blood on Her Shoe*, and before her death in 1959 she authored a highly readable book about the state's old houses called *White Columns in Georgia*. In the meantime her best friend, Margaret Mitchell, had achieved some little success and a man on the *Journal* copy desk named Tom Ripley sold the movies a little something called *They Died with Their Boots on*.

Atlanta writers were off and running. Books came out right and left. Regenstein's advertising chief, Edna Lee, who supported a big, charming family in a high-ceilinged old house in West End, used the time consumed in traveling to and from her job on the streetcar to scrawl into a bunch of nickel notebooks a novel called *Web of Days*. It too was published in New York and sold to the movies for a reported $200,000. Her son, Harry Lee, later a *Constitution* reporter, had already published two novels, *Fox in the Cloak* and *No Measure Danced*, both before his twenty-second birthday. Mother and son followed these books with others, but they subsequently moved away from Atlanta, so their output was no longer local production, although two of Edna's had Atlanta locales—*The Queen Bee* and *The Southerner*.

By the 1940s even the governor, Ellis Arnall, had written a book, *The Shore Dimly Seen*, and was projecting a trilogy.

Foote and Davies, a local printing house, was so impressed by the literary activity in Atlanta that it turned publisher—later to join forces with David McKay Company—and brought out a rash of regional books, including some name ones like *Together*, Katherine Marshall's account of her life with her husband, General George C. Marshall, and some wildly readable ones such as William Campbell's *Big Beverage*, a story of the founders of a soft-drink bottling industry. Local poets were hitting the big time. Daniel Whitehead Hicky, a *Constitution* columnist, had a new volume of verse out nearly every year. Down from the mountains of North Georgia came a gentle, sensitive ballad singer, Herbert Byron Reece, whose book, *Ballad of the Bones* was to be followed by several novels before his suicide a few years ago.

We had book fairs, and everybody's engagement calendar included dropping by a bookstore nearly every day for some dear chum's autographing session. The woods turned out to be full of novelists, and they gravitated toward their kind in Atlanta. Presently there were so many writers in the area the public appetite for autograph parties was sated and more than one novelist, waiting in the wings for fame, was terrified by the story of the party to which one thousand prospective book buyers were invited and *three* came.

Still the writing goes on. Although they are prone to draw nigh to one another for comfort and occasional conviviality, there's no real all-embracing literary set in Atlanta. There's Peggy Gaddis, who lives between Atlanta and Stone Mountain ("two miles from the nearest loaf of bread") and has written 240 books, 150 short stories, 25 to 30 series and seven movies. She doesn't even come to town to shop, much less brave meetings and parties.

Then there's Flannery O'Connor, who lives on a farm one hundred miles to the south just outside Milledgeville, and Lillian Smith, who has a home in the North Georgia mountains and an apartment in town. Both are nationally renowned and accessible. They lecture at the colleges and speak when bidden at the meetings of the Atlanta Writers Club or the Pen Women. Miss Smith's first novel, *Strange Fruit,* was the forerunner of the books about race problems and brought her a storm of criticism and censure from her native state. But the years have softened and sweetened many of her critics and not too many months ago "Miss Lil," as she is called locally was honored at a mass surprise party at the Biltmore Hotel. Since *Strange Fruit* she has written prodigiously and with great success—*Killers of the Dream, The Journey* and others.

When I started this chapter, a friend warned me that I could not, without the most grueling census taking, list all the writers in Atlanta.

"You can spit in any direction," he said, "and you'll hit a writer."

He's right and I don't propose to offer anywhere near a complete list. Trade-paper publishing is a brisk enterprise in Atlanta. The Chamber of Commerce brings out, under the adroit direction of Editor Jim Townsend, a slick beautiful monthly magazine called *Atlanta.* Mrs. William Lewis, a former South Carolina weekly editor, publishes another, *The Georgia Magazine,* in which numerous local writers see their works. The University Press at Athens publishes a quarterly review which occasionally displays the talents of an Atlanta writer and from time to time brings out a book of local author-ship. In addition to the local newspapers and the wire serv-ices, several Georgia newspapers, the New York *Times, News-week* and *Time* and *Life* have bureaus in Atlanta, offering employment to scores of Alexander Woollcott's "ink-stained wretches."

So it wouldn't take a long-distance spitter, as my friend sug-gested, to hit a writer of some kind, probably one of national reputation. For instance, within a few blocks of my apart-ment in Ansley Park there's Margaret Long of *Louisville Sat-urday* and *Affair of the Heart* fame, now editor of the South-ern Regional Council's publication *The New South*; M. H. (Maggie) Davis, who wrote *The Winter Serpent* a year or so back and *The Far Side of Home* this year; Genevieve Holden (Mrs. Charles Pou), author of half a dozen mysteries; and Mary Cobb (Mrs. Owen Bugg), who wrote the novel *Top Dog* a few years back. My immediate circle of friends includes Mrs. Oliver (Ruth) Herbert, a regular and prolific writer for the pulps; Wylly Folk St. John, successful short-storyist; Betsy Hopkins Fancher, whose *Blue River* was a success of several years ago.

Their names come to mind handily, but there are many, many more. Bell Irvin Wiley, an Emory professor, who spe-cializes in the Civil War and whose books *Johnny Reb* and *Billy Yank* were among the first and the best of the collections of letters from the common foot soldier. Marguerite Steed-man, author of *But You'll Be Back* and *Refuge in Avalon*. Elizabeth Stevenson, a quiet young woman who used to work at the library, and who keeps winning prizes with her bio-graphical works: *The Crooked Corridor: A Study of Henry James* (1949), *Henry Adams* (1955) and *Lafcadio Hearn*

(1961). Paul d'Arcy Boles, who writes for an advertising agency by day and turns out novels at night—*Beggars in the Sun, The Streak, Deadline* and others—as well as magazine fiction. Davenport Steward, newspaperman turned publicist, who has half a dozen historical novels to his credit. And there's Tom Ham, one of the freshest and brightest writing reporters the town has ever known. Tom wrote a novel about the Georgia mountains called *Give Us This Valley,* and then he retired from the field to run a series of highly successful restaurants called "The 7 Steers," for which he writes whimsical menus, advertisements and signs urging customers to "Hep stamp out home cookin'."

The closest thing to a register of writers in Atlanta would be in the memories of people like Mrs. Raymond Massey, of the Georgia Writers Association, and Mrs. Walter Slayden, of the Pen Women. Both these organizations have for many years applauded and encouraged the efforts of the writing fraternity, in and out of their own membership. (Mrs. Slayden, the former Thelma Thompson, is herself the author of several books.) The Georgia Writers Association has been rewarding regional writers with cash and citations since 1948, when it was founded by the Atlanta Writers Club at Mrs. Massey's urging. The Pen Women stage a Celebrity Breakfast at the Driving Club each year to honor local citizens who have published books in the last twelve months.

The bookstores are kind to local authors, tendering them little parties if the prospect of a full-fledged autograph shindig is too terrifying for both bookseller and writer. But more important, there's a sort of public enthusiasm for writers and writing that makes even the producer of the dullest and most esoteric tome feel that his words in print are something to celebrate.

One of the all-time gala book parties in Atlanta was given, tongue in cheek, by the wife of a well-loved Atlanta physician, Dr. Murdock Equen, when he authored a chapter in a medical book. She summoned several hundred friends to the Capital City Club for cocktails and they joyfully wrung his hand and spoke their congratulations, although few if any of them could read, much less pronounce, the name of his work.

Religion, Mild and Juicy

CHAPTER XIII

H. L. Mencken called the South the Bible Belt and viewed it as a church-going, hymn-shouting and Scripture-thumping region where fundamentalism and blue laws reigned and the pious drank white lightning in the bathroom.

Atlanta, being the capital of the Deep South, would ostensibly be home plate for that kind of religion.

If it is or ever was, it doesn't seem so to the locals now. Atlantans go to church, it's true. Nothing short of a smallpox epidemic would keep the city's more than six hundred churches from standing-room-only attendance on Sunday and many of them have double sessions. (This serves two purposes. It makes room for all comers and it enables churchgoers who want to go to the lake or the golf course to get an early start.)

Fundamentalism predominates, without a doubt. A 1961 census showed that 37.70 percent of the city's population was

Baptist, 20.45 percent Methodist, 8.89 percent Presbyterian, 5.19 percent Roman Catholic, 2.85 percent Jewish, and the other 24.92 percent "all other denominations," ranging from Episcopalians to Jehovah's Witnesses.

This came as a surprise to some people who regarded Atlanta as the seat of Southern Methodism and assumed that with so much Methodist activity in the area it had to be the predominant denomination.

In many ways the Methodists have had the public eye—and ear. Emory University is a Methodist college with a finger in many civic pies. Due to the benevolence of the Candler family, ardent Methodists all, Emory owns a great deal of real estate. Warren Akin Candler, brother of Asa Griggs Candler, founder of the Coca-Cola Company, was a Methodist bishop and one of the most vocal and most colorful churchmen in the region.

I interviewed Bishop Candler at his home on North Decatur Road on his eighty-fourth birthday, shortly before his death in 1941. He was old and ill, but vestiges of the power and wit which had for more than fifty years dominated the church scene in the South were still present.

Alfred M. Pierce, who wrote the old bishop's biography, *Giant Against the Sky*, called him "master of scorn, ridicule, invective, irony and sarcasm." He set out to be a lawyer, but he also studied theology at Emory College at Oxford, Georgia (the forerunner to the present university and now a junior college). As a result he was licensed to preach, and three months before his eighteenth birthday he was pushed by a classmate into preaching his first sermon.

It must have been a potent experience because, taking the text, "Whatsoever thy hand findeth to do, do it with thy might," young Mr. Candler converted himself. He gave up law forthwith for the ministry. Those who heard him say he was a memorable preacher and a tireless one. Today's fashion for the half-hour sermon would have been abhorrent to him.

"The age of short sermons is the age of shallow piety," he said.

But when he had to sit through a brother preacher's seemingly endless sermon and it came time to announce the closing hymn, Mr. Candler darted a glance full of mischief at the long-winded one and solemnly called for the singing of "Hallelujah, 'Tis Done."

Bishop Candler did not suffer fools gladly, and he was equally merciless with himself. When his members gave him an automobile once and he drove it into the bushes while trying to negotiate his own driveway, a neighbor rushed out and asked him if he was hurt and if she should call the doctor.

"No, call a veterinarian," said the bishop. "If I hadn't been a jackass I wouldn't have been trying to drive that thing."

A short man, five feet, six inches tall, with a massive head and a mighty torso, Bishop Candler was a formidable figure in the pulpit and the timid tried to avoid provoking his wrath. Once an usher asked a woman to take a crying baby from the sanctuary while the bishop spoke. The bishop saw her leaving and he interrupted his sermon to call out, "Sit down, my sister! It's a mighty sorry shepherd that is bothered with the bleating of the lambs!"

The bishop was frequently in conflict with various branches of the Methodist Church. At the peak of some doctrinal dispute, according to Pierce, somebody asked Bishop Candler if he didn't think his opponents were good people.

"Oh, yes," the bishop replied with no great enthusiasm.

The next question was if he didn't think "they will get to heaven."

"Yes," said Candler, "if they don't run past it."

Bishop Candler served as president of Emory University and as chancellor. He was named "First Citizen of Atlanta" by the Chamber of Commerce in 1932 and the Emory theology school now bears his name. He was vigorously opposed to whiskey in any form and although he must have been pleased that his brother's Coca-Cola fortune was poured liberally into Emory, he stoutly maintained that he owned no stock in the company.

"I never owned any stock except a one-eyed pony and a three-teat cow," he said.

Understandably partisan about his own denomination the bishop had no patience with those who wandered into other folds. When he learned that one of his students had married and had joined the Episcopal Church with his wife, the bishop said, "I always knew that if you ever got religion you'd get it in its mildest form."

In common with old-time Methodist evangelists, Bishop Candler believed that a public speech which made no appeal to the emotions was inherently defective.

The greatest exponent of this brand of emotional oratory to parallel Bishop Candler's career in the Atlanta area was the sensational Sam Jones, also a Methodist.

Sam Jones, who lived from 1857 to 1906, like Bishop Candler started out to be a lawyer. He got so far as practicing in the little town of Cartersville, forty miles north of Atlanta, but as he later wrote of himself, he was "bad to drink whiskey."

Latter-day chroniclers say the young lawyer's addiction to spirits wasn't nearly so serious as he pictured it after he quit, but it must have troubled his family because his father extracted a deathbed promise from him that he would give it up "and meet me in Heaven."

The young lawyer turned preacher delivered his first sermon at little New Hope Church near Cartersville, preaching in the place of the pastor, his grandfather, who came down with a throat malady at the last minute one Sunday. After that he must have sensed his own power, because he was committed to the ministry. He preached all over America, and when he died from a heart attack on a train outside Little Rock, there was national mourning.

His body was brought back to Cartersville for the funeral and then transported to Atlanta by special train, which was draped in black and white with a life-sized picture of him on the front of the engine, to lie in state at the capitol for two days. Thirty thousand people filed past his bier to pay tribute to him.

Walt Holcomb, author of his biography, *Sam Jones: An Ambassador of the Almighty*, traveled and preached with Sam Jones for many years. He wrote of his "merry black eyes," his sense of humor and the "crude, rugged, epigrammatic vigor of what he said."

He quoted Jones himself as saying he never attended a theological "cemetery" and summed up his own brand of preaching by saying, "I always wanted to get the juice out of the text. Others may deal in bones and hoofs and horns and that which is dry and tasteless. I always wanted the juice and always wanted to give the juice to others."

He admitted that he was not "a stickler for creeds, nor an

expounder of dogma" but he devoted himself to championing right and denouncing wrong.

One thing he fought hip and thigh (after he himself gave it up) was whiskey.

"Whiskey is a good thing in its place," he said, "but its place is in hell." And another time, "Nobody but a scoundrel will sell whiskey and nobody but a fool will drink it."

The Reverend Mr. Jones was a good administrator and once headed the Methodist Children's Home in Decatur, raising sixty thousand dollars for its support in a brief and eloquent campaign. He was himself a sunny-dispositioned man who liked children. (His son, Paul, was a *Constitution* reporter for many years and two of his grandsons are staff members now—Paul, amusements editor, and Howell, telegraph editor.)

"I have known preachers who looked as sad and solemn as if their father in heaven was dead and hadn't left them a cent," he said.

Once he spoke out against whiskey in a town where liquor interests were powerful and the mayor took his cane to the evangelist. Doffing his clerical dignity, Sam wrested the cane from the man, threw it aside and felled him with his fists.

To the amazed Walt Holcomb he explained, "If I let him whip me, everywhere I went some one-gallused mayor would be jumping on me. I decided to nip that pastime in the bud."

Paul Jones recalls that one of his grandfather's most popular sermons was entitled, "Quit Your Meanness." This was a favorite theme of his. "Most men when they feel mean feel natural," he said. And once in an address to brother preachers he sympathized with them for some of "the animals" in their flock.

"I wonder that some of you preachers do as well as you do," he said, "when I look at the team you have hooked up—a mule, a billygoat, a skunk and a bumblebee . . . the old kicker kicking at everything that comes up, the old butter with his head as hard as a billygoat, the old toper smelling worse than a skunk, and the old long-tongued sister who can sit in the parlor and lick a skillet in the kitchen."

These famous preachers' successors in local pulpits tend to be more sedate and less picturesque. The Presbyterians had for a brief time the famous Peter Marshall at Westminster Presbyterian Church. He met his wife, Catherine, while she was a student at Agnes Scott College, attending his church, and after their marriage they went on to Washington where he gained renown as pastor of the National Presbyterian Church and chaplain of the U. S. Senate. His career has since been delineated in Mrs. Marshall's book *A Man Called Peter* and a movie of the same name, which was largely filmed in Atlanta.

The Reverend Arthur J. Moore, now a bishop emeritus of the Methodist Church, one of the leading churchmen in the country for more than half a century, was recently named "Citizen of the Year" by Atlanta business leaders. Back in the early 1930s the Methodist Church was "short on bishops," as Bishop Moore now tells it, and they sent him to Asia where he became bishop of three million Methodists. He numbered among his flock Generalissimo Chiang Kai-shek and Madame Chiang, who, as a girl, attended the Methodist Wesleyan College in Macon, Georgia. The Chinese couple are still his friends and he visited them in 1960, when he retired.

The Methodist Church got its start in Georgia with the arrival of John and Charles Wesley in Savannah from England with General Oglethorpe's founding British colony. Social reform—later formation of labor unions in England—has long been one of its strong points. Bishop Moore was, with Ralph McGill, one of the founders of the Southern Regional Council, an organization established for the improvement of race relations. Although he later withdrew from the council, Bishop Moore said it was not for lack of conviction and he considers himself and the Methodist Church generally, to be liberal on matters of race.

Bishop Moore was a railroad flagman in Waycross, Georgia, when he was converted. With a young man's zeal he yearned to go immediately to the foreign missionary field. The church board rejected him—twenty years from the time he was to become one of the denomination's really ocean-hopping, globe-circling bishops.

"I understand better today what the board was up against," he now says. "I don't blame them for not sending me."

The rigors of life in the field require a hardy breed of missionary and Bishop Moore thinks Georgia Methodists have produced some notable examples. Miss Mary Cullen White, now in her eighties, is one example of a Georgia woman who served in the Orient with distinction for many years. She was in China when the Japanese invaded it back in the 1930s and she took a group of Chinese women and sought refuge at a church summer place in the hills.

"Some of my people came hurrying to me one day and told me the Japanese Army was even then advancing on Miss Mary Cullen and her charges," the bishop related. "They said, 'Oh, Bishop, what can be done?' I told them I was sorry but that any army that was so reckless as to bother Miss White would just have to look out for itself!"

Miss White must have dealt summarily with the enemy because Bishop Moore saw her recently at a church meeting in this country, wearing a Chinese dress and very homesick for the Orient.

On the whole, local churchmen are inclined to suspect that religion in Atlanta exists, if not in Bishop Candler's "mildest form," at least in a milder form than of yore. Sometimes members of the clergy wonder if with age and dignity the churches lose some of the "juice" which was so important to Sam Jones.

This has occurred to the Methodists and Baptists particularly. Traditionally the churches of the working classes, both denominations run heavily these days to solid citizens, big, beautiful, decorator-done church "plants" with generous budgets and ministers who, far from being tent hoisters and damnation shouters, belong to the Rotary or Kiwanis Clubs, one or more country clubs, and write books and newspaper columns.

Lamar Q. Ball, a colorful old-time newspaperman, once remarked that Atlanta was the only city he ever saw where all the newspaper columnists wanted to be preachers and all the preachers wanted to be columnists.

Morgan Blake, now dead, was one *Journal* sportswriter and columnist who made the trip from press to pulpit on occasion. A self-celebrated reformed drunk, Mr. Blake taught a Sunday School class at the Baptist Tabernacle and frequently took the podium to exhort sinners to repentance.

Most of the switch has been the other way, however. The

ministers have written columns for so many years that a makeup man on one of the newspapers once remarked that he felt his pages looked downright naked without "preacher prose." The *Journal's* most famous was perhaps Dean Raimundo de Ovies of St. Philip's Cathedral (Episcopal), beloved on the lecture platform, a gentle, humorous man who after his retirement put in years of yeoman service counseling alcoholics at the Georgian Clinic.

The *Constitution's* most phenomenally successful "preacher prose" may have come from Dr. Charles Allen, a Methodist minister who has since moved to Texas, who periodically combined his columns in books which were all-out best sellers in this part of the world.

Now the *Journal* has a Methodist, Dr. Pierce Harris, whose big downtown First Methodist Church advertises its services on a billboard with the slogan, "And the Folks Are Friendly." The *Constitution* splits six columns a week among three ministers—Dr. Roy O. McClain, pastor of the biggest church in Georgia, the six-thousand-member First Baptist; Dr. Vernon S. Broyles, Jr., pastor of North Avenue Presbyterian Church, and Dr. Robert Ozmont, pastor of St. James Methodist.

Being a minister in Atlanta is easy, some of today's clergymen point out. Almost without exception, business leaders are active in church and sympathetic to church projects and causes. Church membership is a "must" for those who would seek public office. Even the late Ben Massell, Lithuanian-born immigrant boy who became a multimillionaire by building stores and offices and apartment buildings in Atlanta, was a heavy financial contributor to the Jewish Temple, although he freely admitted he was not a believer. The fact that he made this statement and I quoted it in a newspaper interview raised an unholy stir among readers of the newspaper and Mr. Massell's friends.

Some of the criticism was directed at him.

"Even if it's true," one man said, "I think it was bad taste for him to mention it."

"Even if he *said* it," another chided me, "you should have left it out of the story."

Church-related programs and institutions in Atlanta are many. There's the Methodist Emory University, Presbyterian Agnes Scott College, an old and well-respected school for women in Decatur; Georgia Baptist Hospital; St. Joseph's Infirmary and Our Lady of Perpetual Help Home for terminal cancer patients, both run by the Roman Catholic Church, which also has its parochial schools, among them a new northside high school named Pope Pius X and promptly nicknamed by the high school set, "Pi Hi."

Among the Negro colleges in the Atlanta University Center, Spelman and Morehouse are Baptist and Morris Brown is Methodist. There are two theological seminaries, Columbia, a Presbyterian school in Decatur, and Gammon, a Methodist combine of schools of religion at the Negro university center. One of the biggest orphanages in the country is run by the Baptist Church in Hapeville near the Atlanta Airport and the Methodists operate a children's home in Decatur.

The Atlanta Council of Churches sponsors many of the city's good works, including a chaplaincy program at Grady Hospital, where many young ministers intern in the field of medical ministry. There is a Council of Churches social agency in the Community Chest and the Christmas Bureau, operated from Thanksgiving to Christmas as a clearing house for all Yuletide charities.

The Protestant Radio-Television Center near the Emory campus is an interesting interdenominational project. Here a big staff of professionals work full time producing films and radio tapes for broadcast in all parts of the world. Stars from Hollywood and Broadway frequently come to appear in these productions and recently many of them have been used by the Voice of America.

Of the nineteen million Baptists in America, ten million are Southern Baptists, a group which split with their Yankee brethren at a meeting in Augusta, Georgia, in 1845 over several issues, one being whether slave-owning ministers could be missionaries. Of this ten million, the biggest Protestant denomination in the country, more than 131,000 belong to 160 Atlanta churches.

This doesn't count several-score independent Baptist groups who don't belong to the Southern Baptist Convention. The Baptist, by all accounts, is a ruggedly independent churchman, autonomous in his own congregation, under no compulsion to cotton to or affiliate with any other organization. That's how the term "Hardshell" Baptist came about.

The "Hardshell" originally was a Baptist who was a unit to himself, holding so firmly to the doctrine of the "priesthood of the believer" that he permitted no minister in his church and eschewed all missionary work. There are several "Hardshell" or Primitive Baptist churches in Atlanta, some new ones with beautiful modern churches, and although they vary in their operations some still observe the old foot-washing rites and some cling to the custom of having no minister and no instrumental music in the church.

Contrast this kind of Baptist with the Southern Baptist's impressive Second Ponce de Leon Church. (It started out on Ponce de Leon but has been next door to the Roman Catholic Cathedral of Christ the King on Peachtree for many years.) Second Ponce de Leon has a rich and stylish congregation numbering four thousand members and regularly contributes a quarter of a million dollars to missions.

Baptists as a denomination have been criticized for failure to take a postive liberal stand on racial matters in Atlanta. Some of this criticism, says Jack Hardwell of the denomination's paper, *The Christian Index*, is justified but understandable.

"No one person or organization speaks for a Baptist," he explained. "The convention merely suggests or recommends and individual churches and members are by no means bound by its action. That's why we call our representatives in the convention 'messengers' instead of delegates. They can vote without binding the people back home."

The Christian Index itself has been more outspoken. In times of racial dispute it has repeatedly reminded Baptists that the Christian approach is one of law and order and "respect for the rights and humanity of all races." It fights gambling and illicit liquor traffic tooth and nail. It also campaigned to have a Negro student from Ghana admitted to the Baptist Mercer University in Macon.

The paper is now edited by John Hurt, Jr., and is one of the oldest (founded in 1822) in America. Dr. Louie D. Newton, pastor of the Druid Hills Baptist Church and now in his seventies, edited the *Index* for ten years.

Dr. Newton, sometimes a controversial figure in Atlanta and a particularly strident voice where alcoholic beverages are concerned, is the dean of Baptist preachers in the area and sometimes called "Mister Baptist" by his colleagues. He is a former president of the Southern Baptist Convention and former vice-president of the Baptist World Alliance and in 1953 was named America's "Clergyman of the Year."

He alone among big city ministers flavors his sermons and announcements with old country references, reminiscent of the once popular "protracted meetings" which started and kept going as long as preachers' voices held out and the crowds kept coming.

His is a big city church with around three thousand members, but he still speaks of it as "the Druid Hills meeting house." And summer revival is to his congregation of city people "lay-by meeting."

When Company Comes

CHAPTER XIV

Although it loves visitors and frequently gets exercised over what has come to be referred to as "tourism," a well-paying industry which has replaced cotton and corn as a money crop, Atlanta is not really a tourist town. Its resemblance to a bona-fide tourist place like New Orleans, for instance, is about as close as that of a man who built a better mousetrap to Broadway entrepreneur Billy Rose.

People beat a pathway to our door, all right, but their mission is usually business and not to see the sights. While they are here Atlantans want them to have a good time and diligently stir around, pointing out the resident's routine delights, hoping to more than compensate for the shortage of sight-seeing buses and guides giving step-this-way-folks spiels.

It must work out so the visitor doesn't feel unduly deprived, because I know a long-time resident of Atlanta whose advice to all brides is: "If you're going to live here, my dear, don't have a guest room unless you want it eternally filled. No matter where your relatives and friends are going, Atlanta is on the way."

To some visitors, usually wives accompanying their husbands on a business trip or to a convention, the department stores downtown and at that fabled Peachtree Road shopping center, Lenox Square, are tourist attraction enough. A visiting executive recently reported to his brethren at a convention that his wife had been "lost in Rich's for three days."

"I wonder," he mused aloud, "if anybody has ever sued a department store for alienation of affections."

Groups with special interests are the easiest to entertain. Garden clubbers hit the flower shows and garden tours, of which there are many in the spring and fall. Music lovers, if they are lucky enough to get tickets, aim for the Met's annual spring season or, at the very least, the Symphony or Music Club series. Antiquers will case the local shops and galleries, make the regular Thursday night auctions, but if their timing is right they'll also get to one of the quarterly Southeastern Antiques Shows at the Municipal Auditorium. There are boating shows at the Merchandise Mart and Civil War buffs come primed for centennial fetes and celebrations. Gospel singers have all-night sing fests at the Auditorium and once I lucked into a chance interview with a group of wide-eyed young people, students of a northern morticians' college, who were making their senior class trip to the Atlanta Casket Company and H. M. Patterson's famous undertaking emporium, Spring Hill.

What Atlanta has to offer the visitor obviously depends upon what the visitor is interested in.

The first thing nearly everybody does with a guest is to drive through the northside sections where the more splendid homes are situated. This is gratifying to us hosts, who never tire of seeing how the other, well-heeled half, lives. And I think guests find it interesting because not all cities house their rich people in palaces set in parks.

In the 1920s and 1930s, Atlanta money literally went to the woods. Out on West Pace's Ferry Road and half a dozen others, Norman castles and Italian villas and English manor houses came to what had previously been sourwood thickets, broom-sedge fields and forests of oak, maple and pine. Everybody who built a big house in those days had acreage to show it off and they used it profligately. Landscape design supplemented freehanded nature with fountains and terraces, arbors and rose gardens and statuary.

Some of these old estates are already doomed. One of the great ones, built by Robert F. Maddox, the former banker and onetime Mayor, was sold to the state as a site for a new and totally different Governor's Mansion. The Andrew Calhoun home, an Italian villa called "The Pink Palace" by generations of Atlantans, was set roughly a morning's hike from the road, and Sunday drivers used to park their cars at the big double gates and gaze upon it with awe and admiration. Now, alas, its grounds have been cut up into subdivision lots and the winding roadway to the palace is lined with ranch houses.

There are still many palaces and near-palaces on West Pace's Ferry, Habersham, Wesley, Andrews and neighboring roads—and for as long as they last they are among our town's most reliable attention-getters.

The second thing I try to show every visitor is the Cyclorama in Grant Park.

This curious old painting, housed in its own circular building in the city park, not too far from the elephant house and the rest of the zoo, is an unbeatable combination of art show, sideshow and history lesson. I had lived in Atlanta many years before I got around to seeing it, and then I went in line of duty. Olivia de Havilland, the screen Melanie of *Gone With the Wind*, considered it so memorable she brought her first husband, author Marcus Goodrich, by Atlanta on their wedding trip just to see it. A photographer and I went to the park to cover their visit and I have been going back with visitors on an average of once a year since.

The picture, fifty feet high and four hundred feet in circumference, depicts the Battle of Atlanta. It was painted about twenty years after the battle by a group of German artists and taken on a tour of the United States in the '80s. It dropped from sight for a couple of years and then showed up in Atlanta in 1892, where it was eventually sold at auction to George U. Gress, a citizen who presented it to the city. I don't know what they did with this 18,000-pound behemoth until it got its own building in Grant Park in 1921, but in 1936 the WPA took a hand and, lo and behold, the old picture went three-dimensional and was wired for sound.

The foreground was filled in with blasted tree trunks, broken rails and crossties and plaster figures of soldiers, all so cunningly constructed and lighted that the visitor standing on the platform in the center has a sensation of being in the midst of battle.

The ladies of the Cyclorama staff used to give little speeches explaining the battle action, but a few years ago the whole thing was taped and now the guides simply go along with a little flashlight, directing your eyes to the part of the canvas under discussion as the deep, resonant voice of Don Elliot of the WSB staff tells the story. Then the lights go up and they play "Dixie" and you come blinking out into the sunshine feeling like Scarlett O'Hara the morning after the battle.

This attraction costs one dollar for grownups and fifty cents for children between six and twelve, but you can visit the museum on the ground floor free, looking your fill at relics, uniforms, swords, shells, photographs and letters. Here also is a model of the cruiser *Atlanta*, rebuilt by public subscription after it was torpedoed in the Pacific in World War II, and the marvelous little railroad train, "Texas," which starred in the eighty-seven-mile race so vividly retold in recent years by Walt Disney's *The Great Locomotive Chase*.

Akin to the Cyclorama as a sight and wonder spectacularly and peculiarly Atlanta—that is, not to been seen anywhere else in the world—is Stone Mountain.

Although it is in another county (De Kalb) with another municipality at its base (Stone Mountain, Georgia, once called New Gibraltar), Atlantans have for more than a century had a funny, compulsive attachment to this monstrous old chunk of granite. When nothing much is happening—and sometimes when there's plenty happening—Atlantans do battle over Stone Mountain.

It has been the center of outrageous civic argument, the victim of one national money-grabbing scandal, the object of fervent patriotic hopes and aspirations and, betimes, chipped at, dynamited, carved, hauled off by the trainload, surveyed, landscaped and, above all, climbed.

On any sunny weekend you can find hundreds of families

trudging up Stone Mountain. For years teen-agers have ended their high school dances by racing out to the mountain, taking off their shoes and clambering up its worn gray granite flank. Elias Nour, a refrigerator repairman, has lived his life in the shadow of the mountain and explored it so thoroughly that he is always being called upon to rescue some foolhardy or unwary climber from a cliff or crevice. This started when he was thirteen years old and the score totaled thirty-six rescues not so long ago.

People have been killed in falls from the mountain. Suicides have leaped from it. It was once the favorite rallying ground of the Ku Klux Klan. (Where could you find a better vantage point for burning a cross than a big bare stone pinnacle rising 1586 feet above sea level?) The Venable family, then owners of the mountain, finally stopped these gatherings after one of the KKK's noisier "Konvokations."

Old Stone Mountain has been a variety of things to a variety of people. The Indians who used to hold their council meetings there are said to have looked on the mountain with superstitious awe. General George Washington's aides found it a likely spot for military conference. Quarrymen who shipped out millions of tons of it to build such Atlanta institutions as the Federal Penitentiary, Courthouse, Library and churches, as well as hundreds of post offices all over the United States and in Cuba, have called it "the largest deposit of merchantable granite in the world."

The United Daughters of the Confederacy who started trying to make it a Confederate memorial back in 1915 called it a "custodian of imperishable glory." Geologists have said it was "born in the nether fires of the earth" and older than the Pyrénées, the Rockies or the Himalayas. Frank

Daniel, a *Journal* writer who has observed its misadventures
for nearly half a century, once called it "a memorial to Georgian chicanery." And more recently, Atlanta's Mayor Ivan
Allen, officiating at the launching of a cable car to the sum-
mit, called the mountain the only thing about Atlanta "Sherman didn't burn or the Yankee carpetbaggers cart away."

Periodically, Atlantans retell the history of old Stone
Mountain, relating with relish the apocryphal tale of how it
was sold sight unseen to an Athens, Georgia, man years ago.
When he arrived to claim it he was so shaken by what he
had acquired he quickly swapped it for a mule and a pair of
shoes and went home. An Augusta woman tells how her ancestors bought it for forty dollars and a pony and there's also
the story of an early owner who offered to trade the mountain
for a long-barreled shotgun and a silk handkerchief but could
find no takers.

In any case, records show that Sam and William Venable
bought it for forty-eight thousand dollars in 1887 and it cost
the State of Georgia a cool million dollars "and other valuable
considerations" when it was acquired for a state park in 1959.
For years Scotch and Welsh quarrymen offered the principal
activity on the mountain, but in 1916 the United Daughters
of the Confederacy acquired the steep side for a Confederate
memorial. The Venable family deeded this chunk of the
mountain and some level land in front of it to the UDC
with the stipulation that if a memorial was not completed in
twelve years it would revert to the family.

The memorial, needless to say, was not completed. As of
the year 1963 it is still the subject of debate reported almost
weekly in the newspapers. The sculptor Gutzon Borglum
started the first carving on the mountain, a mammoth, two-

hundred-foot-high procession of men, guns and horses with
Robert E. Lee, Stonewall Jackson and Jefferson Davis riding
in the foreground and columns of Confederate infantry
swinging off in the distance.

World War I interrupted the work, but it was resumed in
1922 with funds raised by an especially minted U. S. half
dollar which the UDC sold for one dollar. In 1924 the head
of General Lee was unveiled with some ceremony—and then
the memorial hit the skids.

Money was going fast, the carving was going slow. Mr.
Borglum was dismissed, and in a rage of righteous indigna-
tion he destroyed his model and fled the city before an in-
junction. Subsequent investigation vindicated the sculptor
and involved the president of the Stone Mountain Association in misuse of funds. Clark Howell, editor of the Atlanta
Constitution, later pointed out that as long as "the Daughters" were running the thing themselves it went fine, but when
a board of Atlanta businessmen took over to help them the
project broke down.

Augustus Lukeman was the second sculptor hired, and he
began by blasting the heads off Lee and Jackson and starting
over. On April 9, 1928, the memorial association issued en-
graved invitations to an unveiling of "General Robert E. Lee
and Traveler" on the sixty-third anniversary of Appomattox.
Two years later Lukeman discontinued work because of lack
of funds, and in 1932 he died.

Time and the weather eroded the unfinished figures.
Weeds grew up at the base of the mountain where a landscaped plaza with a reflecting pool had been planned. People
spoke sadly of "the unfinished memorial" but continued to
climb the mountain, picnic in its shadow and take visitors

to view the carving through a telescope at the dilapidated little concession stand at the base of the mountain, where you could buy Cokes and postcards.

Some citizens, however, never relinquished the dream of having Stone Mountain recognized by the whole world as "the Eighth Wonder," which Georgians have always called it. Scott Candler, for many years the De Kalb County commissioner, secured an option on two thousand acres of the mountain from the Venable heirs and later, as director of the State Department of Commerce, he was able to give impetus to the park plan.

Things have been moving fast since then. The Stone Mountain Park Authority was formed and empowered to issue five million dollars' worth of bonds to make the old mountain "the scenic showplace of the South." A ten-thousand-dollar competition was launched to find an artist to finish the memorial, and a sculptor named Walter Hancock was chosen from a field of nine. Crews moved in to build highways around the mountain, a five-mile scenic railroad, dams and a five-hundred-acre lake.

Members of the authority scouted the state with the idea of assembling in the three-thousand-acre park area everything, both old and new, primitive and civilized, which might interest visitors to the South. By the spring of 1963 they were well along in accomplishing this goal. Home folks trooped out to the mountain by the thousand every fair Sunday to cheer the project on. And as one visitor happily noted, "It's going to be glorious—a sort of cross between Williamsburg, Disneyland and the Grand Canyon."

There's a mountaintop observatory with restaurant, a cable car (Swiss-built and appropriately dedicated by cracking *both* a bottle of Swiss wine and a bottle of Coca-Cola on its prow), a whole antebellum plantation layout, complete with white-columned "great house," overseer's cottage, slave cabins, outbuildings, country store and gardens. These buildings were moved bodily from older sections of Georgia and lovingly rebuilt and furnished with antiques of the period.

There's a side-wheel showboat on the lake, a railroad museum, a game ranch, where you can get a close-up of buffalo and the deer come and eat out of your hand. There's an old car museum, a grist mill where you can buy water-ground meal, picnic areas and campsites.

The aim of the authority is to give the visitor something for his money—if he has money to spend—but to give him something anyhow. Many of the attractions are free, including a battle museum where Sherman's march to the sea is re-fought with lights on a vast relief map. Picnicking and camping and fishing from the bank are all free. And so, of course, is climbing.

As this is written, prices have not been set on many of the attractions, but a trip on the scenic railway costs adults $1.60 and children between the ages of five and eleven years ninety-three cents. Children under five ride free, if accompanied by adults.

The railroad trip is perhaps the most Disneylandish touch of all. The little train, called General II, after that one in *The Great Locomotive Chase*, chugs around the mountain with bell ringing and whistle blowing. Two villages, one patterned with a pioneer North Georgia settlement and the other a make-believe Indian village, have been built on the route, and when the train passes, raids and massacres break out with

musketry cracking and arrows flying. Delighted young passengers are invited to bring their own six-shooters from home
to "help fight off the attackers." These attackers are, of
course, war-painted locals, but they fling themselves into the
fray with satisfying realism.

Stone Mountain is fifteen miles from downtown Atlanta
and the old streetcar which used to career wildly and inex-
pensively out from town has long since vanished. But Atlanta is not a town for walking tours or even bus tours of
the kind you find in New York, San Francisco, New Orleans
and Charleston. Local citizens walk with pleasure, consider-
ing it enough to be abroad in the city, savoring its routine
sight and smells. But unless the downtown restaurants and
stores and theaters are your destination you can count on
covering distances, sometimes great distances, to see the
homes and historic shrines and recreation spots which are beloved by the home folks.

If you don't have a car and don't want to bestir yourself
to get out of the downtown area, you can still have a pleasant-
enough time. On weekdays the state capitol is open
and there's no better place to get a quick briefing on state
history than from monument-reading on the lawn, which, incidentally, happens to be one of the prettiest and best tended
yards in town. (Secretary of State Ben Fortson is so zealous
about velvety lawn and year-round blooming borders that during the bitter winter of 1962–63 when everything froze, he in-
vested in six hundred dollars' worth of green dye to restore
color to the brown grass.) The second floor of the capitol
houses the state's Hall of Fame and although marble busts
and dark portraits of dead heroes are not everybody's dish,

some of us feel one way to appraise a community is to take a look at the men it has most admired.

The third floor of the capitol is given over mostly to its legislative halls—a great show, in season, and free, unless you count the cost to the taxpayer. And the fourth floor has a small museum which never fails to waylay me when I pass. It depicts the state's natural and economic assets with glass cases full of agricultural and geological exhibits, Indian relics and jewel stones, mammoth cotton plants and birds and insects, stuffed animals and snakes.

If you are not a glass-case tourist, a plaque and monument reader, a peerer at portraits, you will know it and skip this. But if you've never been able to tell a mockingbird from a field lark or a rattlesnake from a copperhead, if you're curious about kaolin mines, shrimp boats, pulpwood or Indian pottery, you can spend happy and profitable hours here without cost.

In any case, if you're over that way—and the capitol is in walking distance of every downtown hotel or you can grab the ten-cent shopper's special bus—you might want to drop by the Department of Commerce on the ground floor and fortify yourself with maps, brochures and pamphlets about the rest of Georgia. Mr. Nelson Shipp presides over this department and the visitor who hungers and thirsts after information is his delight.

If I were a visitor with time and a car at my disposal I would make sure to ask Mr. Shipp for one of his tour brochures. He has one called "Four One-Day Tours [from Atlanta] of Georgia's Historic, Scenic and Recreation Spots."

These are well-planned expeditions with mileage and highway numbers carefully set forth. The first one (159 miles round trip) takes in the Warm Springs Foundation of polio fame and, of course, the charmingly simple cottage which was President Roosevelt's "Little White House." This is now a state park and has been preserved substantially as it was the day he died there, April 12, 1945. There's a museum on the grounds with many mementos of his days as President and part-time Georgian. (Cost: one dollar admission for adults; fifty cents for children ages six to twelve. Special rates for groups numbering more than fifteen.)

The Warm Springs tour also includes a trip to President Roosevelt's favorite lookout on Pine Mountain, where he grilled steaks for guests and neighbors; visits to a trio of pretty little towns and two gardens—Callaway Gardens, built as a vacation spot with food and lodging and activities, and Dunaway Gardens, twenty acres of flowers and trees.

The second of these tours heads north through Civil War battlefield country and some remarkable sites of Indian restoration, including New Echota, the capital of the Cherokee Nation and the Etowah Indian Mounds in the mineral belt section near Cartersville (round trip 248 miles).

Tour 3 swings by Stone Mountain to take in Athens, the site of the University of Georgia and several other beautiful little towns which are, like Athens, notable for the high incidence of their Greek Revival architecture. This one brings you back by Conyers, which is about twenty-four miles south of Atlanta and is distinguished in this predominantly Protestant countryside for its exotic neighbors, the Trappist monks. These solemn fellows in their brown cowls came to Georgia from Gethsemane, Kentucky, in 1944 to build a monastery on some cottoned-out land, part of which once belonged to the silent-era screen star, Colleen Moore. Although quiet and unsmiling and foreign to this part of the world, the monks became cherished citizens in this little suburban community. They vote and contribute to charities and run such a model farm it has been an inspiration to their neighbors. Their dairy and bread trucks cover the countryside, distributing rich milk and the fragrant dark brown loaves for which they are famous. They have designed and built a beautiful church where numbers of Atlantans go on Easter and Christmas to sit in the balcony and listen to the ancient Gregorian chants. Visitors are welcome to parts of the monastery, and next to their bread, which I always buy, I like to visit the greenhouse and come away with a few pots of the heart-leafed and silver-edged monastery ivy.

The fourth of the one-day tours covers 218 miles, round trip, and takes you into the mountains, the gold-mining country around Dahlonega, where the first major gold rush began in 1828 and where tourists are still invited to pan for gold. It also covers more battlefields and antebellum homes.

If you have more time to spend and would like to travel farther, the State Chamber of Commerce can fix you up with plans for seven tours which come close to covering the whole varied big state—from the mountains to the sea, from the peach orchards to the vast brooding Okefenokee Swamp on the Florida border.

I think it is typical of Atlanta, but perhaps not exclusive in these days of fast freeways and winged traffic, that its all-embracing civic pride reaches so far out into the state. The lakes, Allatoona and Lanier, are by no means Atlanta lakes. The closest their shores come to Atlanta is about thirty miles, but every weekend of the summer thousands of Atlantans are at one or the other of them water-skiing, swimming, sailing, houseboating, fishing.

The mountains seem closer because on certain afternoons when the atmosphere is right if you look from a viaduct or any other open space in downtown Atlanta you can see where they begin with the blue shape of Kennesaw against the sky. And when you head north from the city limits, before you are even out of the county, there are whole ranges of mountains stretched out against the horizon in indigo humps and peaks. I am enchanted with the mountains, a section of the state which, until the roads opened up and the power lines came in the 1930s, was virtually untouched by the twentieth century.

Today many Atlantans have weekend or summer places in the hill country and are within reach of the still-secluded hollows and coves where old ways of life and old skills still prevail. Change has come, of course, and the little mountain towns have as many Rexall drugstores and as much neon and pink asbestos siding as little towns anywhere.

But if you wander from the main thoroughfares you can find cabin-made, handloomed pretties to admire and sometimes buy. There are still old-time artisans making "settin' chairs" and bottoming them with split white oak, still potters who will "throw" you a churn or a fat cream pitcher on their own wheel and fire them in a kiln which turns Georgia clay from plum red to muted brown or blue.

All across the top of the state there are roads leading through unbelievably beautiful valleys and over swift-running streams lined in springtime with banks of rosy mountain laurel and rhododendron. There are lookouts and picnic spots and a few old-time country inns where the food is still served family style and platters of fried chicken, ham and red-eye gravy and country steak circulate up and down the table with platoons of homegrown vegetables, hot biscuits, cornbread, homemade butter and buttermilk and a minimum of three kinds of honey and six kinds of preserves.

Because the Indians so recently inhabited this country—they were driven west in the infamous "Trail of Tears" in 1834—Atlanta children are perhaps the premier Indian artifact collectors in the eastern half of the nation. If you don't find Indian arrowheads and shards of Indian pottery in your own backyard you don't have to travel far to find them. In the last few decades there has been a big effort to restore the remnants of Indian civilization. The Ocmulgee National Monument with mounds and a strange council house in Macon (one hundred miles to the south) are famous. The Etowah Mounds near Cartersville (forty miles to the north) are part of a state park.

New Echota, capital of the peace-loving, highly intelligent and agrarian Cherokee Nation, has been undergoing research and restoration by a team of archeologists for several years. (This is near Calhoun, seventy miles north.) And the home of the Scotch-Cherokee chieftains, James and Joseph Vann, is an unfailing marvel to visitors who thought all Indian chiefs lived in wigwams. This is an elegant brick house, modified Georgian in design, planned for the Vanns by a European architect and handsomely furnished with European imports about 1804. The Georgia Historical Commission and Murray-Whitfield County Historical Society saved the old house from destruction by time and vandals a few years ago and restored it to its former glory with its elaborate carvings, cantilevered stairway and wainscoting painted in the colors of the North

Georgia landscape—blue sky, red clay, green trees and yellow ripened grain.

The Vann House, about ninety miles north of Atlanta, is open daily to tourists for a small fee.

There are numbers of Atlantans, of course, who never think of wandering so far afield. They are content to live in city apartments, perhaps one of the new ones which are rearing up among downtown office buildings these days. They can pass up the daisy-starred meadows of the hill country for flowers blooming on traffic islands or in the Citizens and Southern Bank's window boxes. They might drive occasionally to Smyrna, just over the line in Cobb County, to eat country victuals at Aunt Fanny's Cabin, a real old slave shack which has been meticulously kept slanty-shanty primitive by its canny owner, Harvey Hester, with hot hoecake type cuisine and pickaninnies singing and the whole place knee-deep in visiting movie stars and other celebrities.

This type Atlantan doesn't like to buck traffic, and he doesn't figure he has to, to see some pretty satisfactory sights. After work he joins an increasing number of diner-outers who "go upstairs to eat." He catches a fast express elevator to the "Top o' Peachtree" on the thirtieth floor of the Bank of Georgia Building or to the roof of the Merchandise Mart (called "Top of the Mart," what else?) to watch—over a drink and dinner—the sun set on the blue hills to the north and the lights come on in the city below.

Either way, I say, you can't lose.

"Singing Hymns and Balling the Jack"

CHAPTER XV

Newcomers to Atlanta are never sure when they begin to notice it, but there comes a moment, a little space of quiet, when you suddenly realize you are hearing Atlanta's heartbeat.

It could happen in the daytime. But it's likely to happen in the middle of the night when the surf-like pounding of traffic on Peachtree Street has slowed to a meek, ebb-tide whisper. Or it may be that you have been jerked from sleep by the wail of fire sirens or the shrill and officious keening of Grady Hospital's diminutive picture-book ambulance. (The city has a big ambulance or two, but for reasons of economy Grady's Superintendent Frank Wilson tried out a remodeled Ford panel truck a few years ago and found that it operated so efficiently that his junior-size vehicle, careening urgently through traffic at a rock 'n' roll gait, is still first out on all calls.)

Whatever gets your attention, whether it is one of these sharp and imperative sounds or merely that you are wakeful, there will be a time when you first hear the sound behind the sounds of Atlanta. There will be a time when you are aware of a deep low beat, rhythmic as breathing, repetitious as a Bach fugue.

This is the sound of Atlanta's trains.

The city is bound around and crisscrossed with railroad tracks, and no matter what else is happening there are always trains moving, cars coupling, switch engines bustling about the yards like suburban housewives too intent on the duties of home to chafe at the clothesline tether of domesticity. Over and above these steady workaday noises there is a recurring theme, the sweet lifted halloo of an arriving freight, coming in from Chicago with snow on its top, the barnyard-fragrant "Pork Chop Special" pulling a load of pigs to the packing-house siding, the deep-throated peal of a fast passenger heading north with time to make up.

Atlanta is the largest railroad center in the South, with seven systems operating thirteen main lines through the city. More than two hundred and fifty merchandise and package cars originate in and move out of Atlanta daily, and the Railway Express Agency transports in and out of Atlanta more express shipments per capita than any other city in the United States—an average of five thousand cars per month.

As Sherman wrote after the war: "Atlanta was like my hand. The palm was the city or hub. The fingers were its spokes—in this case the railroads. I knew that if I could destroy those railroads, the last link of the Confederacy would be broken."

The railroads which brought down fire and destruction on its head also helped in its rebuilding. And although recent years have taken a toll in passenger trains, causing old Atlantans to mourn, the old affection for railroads and railroading is still with us. Old-timers are not reconciled, of course, to the passage of the steam engine—no more than the old-timers before them were reconciled to the loss of the famous old woodburners who employed firemen, engineer and wood-passer in the cab and are said to have screamed like souls in torment when they were converted to coal. (This screaming, very real and traceable to mechanical causes, is said to have terrified people as far as forty-five miles from the railroad tracks in the late '70s. The converted engines were called "the screaming girls.")

The loss of the steam whistle is both deeply personal and civic, for most Atlantans grew up on stories of the virtuosity of engines and engineers the way lovers of the Met know the special nuances of a Caruso or a Galli-Curci. And to have Atlanta's steam whistles replaced by the mechanical whistles of the diesel engine was a municipal calamity on a par with having every mockingbird in Piedmont Park struck dumb in his prime.

Still, Atlantans love the railroads and the trains and band themselves into what amounts to fan clubs dedicated to the adulation of the Iron Horse. The success of old 290 is an example.

A few years ago E. M. Ivie, a retired Southern engineer and dean of a little group of railroad fans who gather daily at Union Station to bask in the sweet familiarity of railroad sights and sounds, became alarmed that coming generations might never see or hear a steam engine. Mr. Ivie's alarm spread to Leo Aikman, columnist for the Atlanta *Constitution*, and from Leo it fanned out into the state, reaching epidemic proportions. Poor, ignorant children, mourned the railroad devotees, to be reared in deprivation and silence unbroken save by the crude sounds of the jet and diesel age.

They immediately launched a movement to get a proper engine. Not a "cute" historic relic like the famed "Texas," which is in the Civil War museum at the Cyclorama in Grant Park, but a sleek and powerful modern engine. J. Clyde Mixon, president of the Atlanta and West Point Railroad, came forward. His line would contribute an engine they had planned to scrap—the noble 290, which was in main-line passenger service between Atlanta and Montgomery from 1926 to 1954.

The city accepted the train and immediately made plans for placing it on display at Lakewood Park. But the problem of getting the engine from the nearest railroad to the park, a distance of several miles, temporarily baffled Messrs. Ivie and Aikman and others who led the movement. After all, the railroad was sacrificing the scrap value of the engine, a staggering sum of seventy thousand dollars. It could hardly be expected to lay a track to move it. The City Parks Department knew nothing about moving trains.

Leo Aikman cast about for somebody who did know the subject. A luncheon companion suggested the Army—and a few weeks later with flags flying and bands playing and hundreds of excited citizens there to cheer them on the boys of the 836th Engineers Battalion (heavy construction) of the U. S. Army Reserves moved old 290, a few rails at a time, out Pryor Road to Lakewood Park. When the Southeastern

Fair opened some weeks later, she had been wired for sound and was the hit of the exposition.

Visitors are sometimes puzzled to hear Atlantans speaking of "catching the Nancy to Savannah" or "riding the Man to Columbus." Far from being a brand of civic jive talk these references have their roots in the town's history.

The "Nancy to Savannah" simply refers to the Central of Georgia's streamliner, Nancy Hanks II, and the "Man to Columbus" is another Central shoppers and commuters special, the Man o' War. Both were named for racehorses.

When the Nancy Hanks service to Savannah was reinstated in the late 1940s after an intermission of fifty-odd years, the Central of Georgia found it expedient to take an ad to remind customers that the new streamliner had been named for one of America's most glamorous trains, Nancy Hanks I. And *that* Nancy had been named for one of the swiftest trotting horses in the world.

"Then you *didn't* name the train for Abraham Lincoln's mother?" I said to a railroad man, disappointed that a little story I'd had in mind had blown up.

"Oh, was that *her* name?" asked the railroad executive mildly. "How fast could she run?"

My information on the track performance of Mrs. Lincoln (née Hanks) was sadly lacking, but the railroad official more than made up for it with figures on the other Nancy Hanks. The racehorse, for instance, a six-year-old bay mare, broke the world's trotting record in 1892 with 2:04 a mile, holding it until 1894 when a horse named Alix dethroned her by a quarter of a second. But in the meantime the Central had named a magnificent train in honor of the dazzling trotter, Nancy

Hanks—the first complete train in America to be given a name, although engines had been christened before.

The Nancy was placed in service between Atlanta and Savannah on January 22, 1893, and all of Georgia swelled with pride. Deducting time for stops, she made the 294-mile run to the coast in six hours!

She was royal blue trimmed in gold leaf from her cow catcher to her tail light with likenesses of the horse blown into the frosted-glass panels of the coaches. Even the engine and tender were blue and gold and the crew, although wearing the railroad man's traditional blue denim, had specially cut jackets instead of overalls and blue and gold colored leather caps with the name "Nancy Hanks" emblazoned on the bills.

According to Historian Garrett, who is also a railroad fan, the conductor, B. J. (Handsome Barney) Cubbedge was a fitting equerry for this elegant equipage. He wore a white vest with pearl buttons and when he took up a ticket he lifted his hat with a sweeping bow and made a pretty speech of thanks.

All along the line the country people went out of their way to "see the Nancy go by" and even in the more blasé circles in Atlanta a favorite Sunday afternoon entertainment called for driving out to Fort McPherson for the same—"to see the Nancy go by."

They even made up a song which Mr. Garrett quotes:

> *Some folks say the Nancy can't run*
> *But stop! Let me tell you what the Nancy done:*
> *She left Atlanta at half past one*
> *And got to Savannah at the setting of the sun.*
> *The Nancy she run so fast*
> *She burnt the wind and scorched the grass!*

Unhappily, the Nancy ran so fast she also "scorched" vast numbers of cattle and hogs and was so glamorous nobody wanted to ride any other train. So after fighting this double handicap for seven months the Central regretfully retired the first railroad Nancy. At the close of World War II the present Nancy, a modest streamliner built to accommodate shoppers and commuters at budget fares, was placed in service.

As the railroads gave Atlanta birth and have shaped her history, so have they contributed to her social life. Mrs. Mulligan, wife of a railroad laborer, gave the town's first party, you recall, and in 1842 the citizens of Terminus laid aside their duties and took off to cheer the departure of the first Western and Atlantic train for Marietta. After that, such ceremonies occurred with a fair amount of regularity, but Atlantans never became jaded by the sight of arriving or departing trains.

On a summer day now the old Bankhead Avenue bridge overlooking Inman Yards draws family cars packed with children, come to wave at the trains.

Wherever old-timers gather, the talk is well seasoned with references to such trains as "The Goober," the Georgia Railroad's Atlanta-to-Social-Circle special, which was taken off in 1930. It got its name because, according to local raconteurs, tons of goober peanuts were consumed between Social Circle and Atlanta and the aisles were knee-deep in shells. The Air Line Belle, which ran between Atlanta and Toccoa from 1879 to 1931, was famous because it made thirty-nine stops in its ninety-three-minute run.

The men who drove the trains were colorful, and some of them still meet daily with Mr. Ivie and other retired railroaders in the Union Station waiting room.

David J. Fant is in his nineties and as late as 1958 was in demand as a speaker at church meetings. He began preaching while he was an engineer, taking as his credo the Biblical admonition, "Trust in the Lord." Uncle Dave or Daddy Fant, as he was sometimes called, drove a beautifully groomed mountain-type locomotive on the Southern. Its front was ornamented with a picture of an open Bible, across which were emblazoned the words: "Holy Bible. Thy Word is Truth. John 17:17."

Mr. Fant was careful to kneel in prayer before every run, and chroniclers of the day called his 153-mile run a "153-mile prayer and sermon." He even prayed for the notorious Bill Miner gang when four of its members flagged him down at White Sulphur Springs, Georgia, and robbed his train of $127,000 in cash, which was being transported between New Orleans and New York. The robbers were caught and jailed within a week and Daddy Fant called on them in their cells and knelt and prayed with them.

All along the line between Greenville, South Carolina, and Atlanta his fans marked his passage and marveled at his speed. In the fashion of the day they committed his feat to rhyme:

We can tell by the way she'll roar and rant
If the man at the throttle is Daddy Fant!

One night the engineer was making up time and, as Charles H. Dickey wrote in the Atlanta *Journal* magazine in 1935: "He turned the steam onto the pistons until the white drive wheels revolved so rapidly they all but seemed to be standing still. The fireman, yelling across the end of the boiler, said, 'Daddy, ain't we batting 'em up too fast tonight?' "

From the other side of the reeling cab the engineer intoned sonorously: "Trust in the Lord!"

It was the era of the railroad evangelist, who sang hymns as he broke new speed records. Freight engines were called "jacks" and many an engineer was famed for "singing hymns and balling the jack."

An older and ill-fated contemporary of Daddy Fant's was Samuel T. (Preacher) Watkins of the Atlanta-Birmingham run, who was to die in 1921 in the wreck of the Kansas City Special near Anniston. He, too, liked the credo, "Trust in the Lord," and had it painted on his cab. He visited jails, taking his brand of rugged railroading religion to shut-ins, and he knelt and prayed before each trip.

Like Daddy Fant he was a speedster who sometimes frightened his crew as he drove his engine in the hills of Alabama. On one such run his fireman pleaded with him to slow down and he replied easily, "Don't worry. You've got nothing to fear. The Lord's on here with us."

"Maybe he is, Cap'n," said the skeptical fireman, "but He musta got on at Anniston because He sho ain't had time since!"

Most of the doleful old railroad ballads which made the night mawkishly delicious for those gathered around the phonographs in country parlors in some way touched on the lives of Atlanta citizens. These include such tearjerkers as "Ben Dewberry's Final Run," "Wreck of the Royal Palm Express" and, of course, the classic "Wreck of Old 97."

This song, written by David Graves George of Gretna, Virginia, relates the sad saga of a fast mail express which operated through Atlanta between New York and New Orleans, southbound only. Daddy Fant took the 97 out of Atlanta, but, as music lovers will remember, it was Engineer Joseph A. (Steve) Broady who was bringing her south the day of the wreck.

As the song has it:

They gave him his orders at Monroe, Virginia,
Saying, "Steve, we're 'way behind time,
This is not 38 but it's old 97;
We must put her in Atlanta on time!"

And then several quivering stanzas later:

He was going down grade at ninety miles an hour
When his whistle broke into a scream.
He was found in the wreck with his hand on the throttle,
A-scalded to death by the steam.

To be "on time" was a matter of sacred honor to the old engineer. There was a certain do-you-want-to-live-forever insouciance about their insistence on it. An engineer named Tom Russ, who hauled passenger trains between Atlanta and Macon, had the extra challenge of making up time or, as they put it, "snatching territory," on a short run.

Once when he had time to make up he is said to have worked his engine with a low reverse roar at her stack "as though her insides were coming out" and left town "with the ten-wheeler snorting like a bull." As he passed under White-hall Street viaduct he was "shooting skyrockets out of sight."

A few miles out, a cautious conductor signaled him to slow down. Engineer Russ brought his train to a full stop, got out, walked back to the passenger cars, snatched open a door, found the conductor and addressed him thus: "Listen here, you buggy-rider, if I can stay on that engine up yonder, you certainly can ride the cushions back here! Grab a hold—I'm going to Macon *on time!*"

He did, too, his biographers noted with satisfaction.

During World War II the movement of troops revived the flagging importance of trains. For Atlantans that importance was abundantly underscored. Franklin D. Roosevelt, who may go down in history as the last of the train-riding Presidents, frequently passed through on his way to the Little White House seventy-five miles south of Atlanta at Warm Springs.

Moving a Presidential Special is always a sticky assignment for a railroad, and the Southern's task was magnified by the war. The possibility that an attempt might be made to bomb the President's train was ever present in railroad men's minds. As a precaution the Presidential train was sheathed with armor plate on its bottom side next to the tracks and smaller and heavier doors were installed on the President's car.

So concerned was the railroad with keeping the President alive it could not foresee the special problem the narrow door would present if he died. While a sorrowing world was still stunned with the news of President Roosevelt's death on April 12, 1945, crews from Atlanta had to be rushed to Warm Springs to deal with a matter of distracting practicality. The door, large enough for a living man, was too small to admit the man in his coffin.

Railroad workers, many of whom knew him personally and loved him, put aside their grief to work far into the night widening the aperture so the President's coffin could be placed aboard without difficulty the next day.

At 10:15 AM on Friday, the thirteenth of April 1945, the train moved out from the little flagstop station at Warm Springs. Drawn by two locomotives with bells mournfully clanging, the train that had brought him to his vacation home so many times bore the President back to Washington for the last time. Between Warm Springs and Atlanta crowds of silent, sorrowing people lined up along the railroad tracks to see the train go by.

In Atlanta crowds were of course denser, and at Terminal Station Mayor Hartsfield boarded the train briefly to speak to Mrs. Roosevelt and to present a basket of flowers from the people of Atlanta to their famous part-time neighbor. The next day the *Constitution* ran what had been one of the President's favorite photographs—a picture of him waving jauntily from a train window on one of his early trips through Atlanta. (It was taken by Kenneth Rogers, whose pictures also illustrate this book.)

Crimes committed aboard trains keep railroad detectives more than routinely engrossed, but the most sensational crime to involve the railroads is the still-unsolved murder of a handsome opera singer named John Garris on April 21, 1949. Garris, a German-born tenor, who sang here with the Metropolitan Opera Company, was found shot to death in an alley blocks from the railroad yards the morning after the Met had finished its four-day spring engagement here.

Garris had boarded the Met special train shortly before midnight, stowed his luggage away and told fellow singers he was going to play cards awhile. But the train pulled out without him and Atlanta police and railroad detectives who flew to Alabama to intercept the train and question members of the Met company, still don't know what happened to entice Garris from the train and to his death.

He was found with a bullet wound near his heart, laid out

in a wet cold alleyway in what police said was "a neat, almost tender way." His coat, unmarked by bullet or by blood, was found on a florist's rubbish heap two blocks away. The valuables and money on his person were undisturbed.

It is a crime railroaders still talk about when night settles down on the yards and the lonesome cry of a long-gone freight moves them to think of life and death and their mysteries.

Oh, you hear the cries of the trains at night wherever you sleep in Atlanta. You feel the pulse of the big engines sometimes in the daytime when you move about downtown. And it may take you a long time to listen and hear in it again the brawling laughter of the Irish right-of-way builders, the bravado of that pushing, growing frontier town, the bloody battles that were fought over the railroads, the corny ballads, the shrill and biggity noises of commerce. But once you hear it, you know it for what it is—Atlanta's heartbeat.